CONGRESS IN CRISIS: POLITICS AND CONGRESSIONAL REFORM

NEW FRONTIERS IN AMERICAN POLITICS SERIES

L. Harmon Zeigler, Jr., General Editor
University of Oregon

CONGRESS IN CRISIS: POLITICS AND CONGRESSIONAL
REFORM
Roger H. Davidson, David M. Kovenock (Dartmouth College)
Michael K. O'Leary (Syracuse University)

FORTHCOMING VOLUMES:

WHO WILL RULE THE SCHOOLS? A CULTURAL CLASS
CRISIS
Robert E. Agger (McMaster University, Canada)
Marshall N. Goldstein (McMaster University, Canada)

POLITICAL SCIENTISTS AT WORK
Oliver Walter (University of Illinois)

Wadsworth Publishing Company, Inc., Belmont, California

CONGRESS IN CRISIS: POLITICS AND CONGRESSIONAL REFORM

ROGER H. DAVIDSON
Dartmouth College

DAVID M. KOVENOCK
Dartmouth College

MICHAEL K. O'LEARY
Syracuse University

Wadsworth Publishing Company, Inc., Belmont, California
Hawthorn Books, Inc., Publishers, New York

THIRD PRINTING: OCTOBER 1969

L. C. Cat. Card No.: 66–23795

Printed in the United States of America

Published simultaneously by Hawthorn Books, Inc.,
Publishers, New York.

NEW FRONTIERS IN AMERICAN POLITICS SERIES

Political science is a changing discipline, but the changes that are taking place are not very different from those that took place in other social sciences a good many years ago. Briefly, political scientists are becoming interested in empirical (some would say "causal") theory and are seeking the appropriate methodologies that will enable them to develop reliable descriptions of recurring patterns in political life. The nature of the articles that are published in professional journals and monographs, which are no longer the exclusive property of university presses, attest to the general improvement of the discipline. Scholars are beginning to be a little self-conscious about using the term "behavior" as though it designated a specific and unique "branch" of political science.

Graduate education in political science is reflective of this trend. Most departments of political science require that their students acquire a level of sophistication in statistics and research design that would have been considered extreme as late as ten years ago. Thus, a majority of graduate students, rather than a minority as was formerly the case, begin their teaching careers with an appreciation for the importance of a systematic study of political life.

However, one must question the extent to which undergraduate students are exposed to political science research —as it is being conducted today. After all, very few under-

graduate students, even if they are political science majors, go to
graduate school; and the proportion of political science students
who are aware of new developments in research technique or new
explorations of "old" substantive areas is probably unfortunately
small. Although each year sees the appearance of more texts that
rely heavily upon recently published material, one frequently hears
the argument that much of the current research is over the heads
of undergraduates and must be distilled and compressed to be useful.

It is the assumption of this series that a fruitful way to introduce
students to political science research is to let them read it for themselves. They can see the problem faced by the researcher, judge the
validity or logic of the methods, evaluate the extent to which evidence
is supportive of the conclusions, and formulate some idea of the
nature of social research. There is no reason why the pedagogical
assumptions of undergraduate instruction should differ from those
of the graduate program. If there are facts of political and social
life worth knowing, all students should be made aware of them.

L. Harmon Zeigler, Jr.
Series Editor

University of Oregon

CONTENTS

TABLES AND FIGURES

FOREWORD

A. S. MIKE MONRONEY

Congressional reform has been a topic of major interest since the beginning of our government. Our Founding Fathers envisioned a blending of powers among the three coordinate branches. Since that time, a spirited and usually healthy rivalry has taken place in our tripartite system for the sharing of public-policy responsibilities. Scholars have searched for almost two hundred years to ascertain how well Congress is able to meet its constitutional responsibilities. This book is another major contribution to the quest.

Twenty years ago I had the privilege of participating in a major congressional reform. As a result of the Legislative Reorganization Act of 1946, our committees are far better organized and staffed. We took a major step forward in recognizing that our capacity to cope with modern-day problems was directly related to our willingness to organize for the task.

But the technological advances of the past twenty years have put massive new demands on the legislative machinery. The nature of the problems we now study—scientific, economic, and social—would have appeared to be excerpts from a science-fiction magazine when the Legislative Reorganization Act of 1946 was passed. Once again, we face the necessity of finding the organizational tools to reach well-con-

---

The Honorable A. S. Mike Monroney, United States Senator from Oklahoma, is Co-Chairman of the Joint Committee on the Organization of the Congress.

sidered judgments on major public-policy problems or of suffering
the diminution of congressional influence.

And the stakes are high. Our Congress is the envy of free men the
world over. Our natural allies have always been those nations in
which the people have a meaningful opportunity to express their
viewpoint in their government. Today, the people of emerging nations look to us to determine if representative democracy really
works in a complex and turbulent modern world.

This book is a practical analysis of congressional attitudes on reform and a chronology of recent efforts at congressional reorganization. It has the major virtue of recognizing Congress for what it is
—a political institution of elected office holders of diverse constituencies and a variety of philosophies. It avoids the pitfall of useless
theorizing on how Congress might function if it were a different kind
of institution. Instead, it dispassionately assesses the likelihood of
reform with the current composition of both bodies.

I am—as the authors indicate—a believer that congressional reform is a mosaic of many building blocks rather than a single,
spectacular alteration of the power structure. I do not believe that
a strong executive requires a weakened legislature—or that a
strengthened Congress means a more passive Presidency. I believe
we are best served when all branches of government are strong and
responsive to public needs. Perhaps I am also a little more optimistic
than the results of the authors' survey would justify. But I firmly
believe that the world's most important legislature will not permit
itself to drift away from the needs of the people it serves.

Washington, D.C.

DEDICATION:
to R. K. H.
S. K.
D. R. M.
and D. B. T.

ACKNOWLEDGMENTS

Many individuals and organizations have assisted in bringing this research to its present stage of development. We especially wish to recognize the many scholars, journalists, Congressmen, and staff aides who contributed their valuable time and endeavored to answer our oftentimes puzzling queries with patience and insight. Especially valuable were the interviews we conducted during 1963–1964 with 118 members of the House of Representatives and numerous staff assistants. Several groups, including the Democratic Study Group and the Republican Task Force on Congressional Reform and Minority Staffing, added valuable quali-

tative information on the recent history and politics of reform.
Though we have pledged anonymity to all of these persons, we do
not hesitate to say that this is their book in a very meaningful sense.
We hope that our report may in some small measure repay their
generosity to us.

The Public Affairs Center of Dartmouth College has underwritten
our work from its inception; and the Center's able director, Professor Gene M. Lyons, has been an unfailing source of understanding, encouragement, and intelligent criticism. The Public Affairs
Center also provided a forum for the initial report of this research:
the first annual Orvil E. Dryfoos Conference on Public Affairs in
March 1964.

Our undergraduate research assistants, William G. Hamm, James
M. Hollabaugh, and Gerald G. Paul, made important contributions
to this volume. In addition, perhaps a score of Dartmouth students
volunteered their services in various phases of data collection and
analysis. We are happy to record our debt to these lively and capable young people.

The public-opinion materials recorded in Chapter 2 were made
available through the cooperation of Professor Philip K. Hastings,
Director of the Roper Public Opinion Research Center, Williamstown, Massachusetts, and Louis Harris of Louis Harris & Associates,
New York City.

During our Washington sojourns we were beneficiaries of the
warm hospitality and professional facilities of the Brookings Institution. We particularly wish to thank Dr. George A. Graham,
Director of Governmental Studies at Brookings, for his encouragement and cooperation.

Charles O. Jones, Donald R. Matthews, James A. Robinson, and
Harmon Zeigler reviewed the manuscript in its entirety and made
numerous helpful suggestions. At the Wadsworth Publishing Company, Robert Gormley, Richard Kuhn, and their staffs managed to
transform the laborious process of manuscript preparation into a
rewarding phase of our work. In particular, our editor, James
Arntz, was ruthless enough with our prose to have improved this
volume immeasurably.

Finally, we wish to acknowledge two personal debts: to our
families, whose forbearance made this volume possible; and to
our graduate advisors, to whom this volume is dedicated. Though
only one of these men played a direct role in the preparation of the

research, we should like to view this dedication as symbolic of the ongoing character of scholarly endeavor.

Needless to say, we willingly absolve these individuals and organizations of responsibility for any of the facts or conclusions reported herein—an absolution they will no doubt greet with some relief.

R. H. D.
D. M. K.
M. K. O.

Hanover, New Hampshire

INTRODUCTION: THE DILEMMA OF REFORM

Hardly anyone these days needs to be told that the American Congress is a uniquely compelling object of research. Compared with the decision-making processes in the executive or judicial branches, legislative decision making, however complex, is singularly visible to the nonparticipant observer. Additionally, the characteristics of Congress—as a group of interacting political men—have recently yielded to the probing of analytic tools borrowed from the developing behavioral sciences. Concepts derived from such diverse sources as organization theory, role analysis, and small-group analysis have proved useful in developing an understanding of legislative behavior.[1]

Another reason for studying Congress is that it offers a matchless strategic site for viewing the larger American political system. Capitol Hill is a meeting ground for most of the persistent forces of local and national politics. Here the crises of Berlin or Vietnam are juxtaposed with the demands and prejudices of Kalamazoo or Walla Walla. Public policy cannot be understood apart from the pres-

[1] See Robert L. Peabody, ''Organization Theory and Legislative Behavior: Bargaining, Hierarchy and Change in the U.S. House of Representatives'' (a paper presented at the 1963 annual meeting of the American Political Science Association, New York City, September 4–7, 1963); John C. Wahlke, Heinz Eulau, William Buchanan, and LeRoy C. Ferguson, *The Legislative System* (New York: John Wiley, 1962); and the readings collected in *New Perspectives on the House of Representatives*, eds. Robert L. Peabody and Nelson Polsby (Chicago: Rand-McNally, 1963).

1

sures that are exerted and absorbed in the legislative arena.

A final reason for studying Congress—and the particular motivation for this book—is the intense debate in recent years over the very future of legislative institutions. Students of government are universally in agreement with David B. Truman's observation that "the twentieth century has been hard on legislatures."[2] The American Congress has struggled manfully against the anti-parliamentary dynamics of our age, but many scholars have concluded that it is fighting a losing battle.

Whatever one's feelings about the future of parliamentary bodies, the controversy surrounding congressional institutions and practices is indicative of policy demands and developments that are changing the complexion of our political system. When one intelligent and articulate Senator labels Congress "the sapless branch," can there be much doubt that the question of congressional reform deserves systematic analysis?

The Limits of Rational Problem Solving

Debate over the quality of congressional responses to our changing environment has produced, since World War II, a veritable flood of speeches, articles, books, and foundation studies. Many leading scholars have contributed their views on congressional reform— some in response to the work of the 1945 and 1965 Joint Committees on the Organization of the Congress. The insights of many thoughtful members of Congress have also contributed to the debate. And countless editorial writers, classroom teachers, and citizens have sought to arouse public awareness of the issues.

Contributions to this debate have been marked invariably by high purpose—and often by perspicacity. Too frequently, however, the reformers' premises concerning the proper functions of Congress remain unarticulated, or indistinct, or even contradictory. And, if articulated, their premises are often found to be the servants of highly particularized policy aims. Moreover, reformist thinking often displays a surprising naiveté about the probabilities and the mechanisms for institutional reconstruction within the American political system.

2 David B. Truman, *The Congressional Party: A Case Study* (New York: John Wiley, 1959), p. 1.

The conventional notion of reform implies an orderly progression from premises to conclusions to implementations. Although this model may be appropriate for describing one's intellectual processes in a number of problem-solving situations, its requirements are too demanding for application to such large political decision-making structures as legislatures. Under this model of rational problem solving, congressional reform would be effected in somewhat the following manner:

1. Everyone—or at least a considerable majority—would agree on the functions which Congress should be expected to fulfill.
2. Having agreed upon the goals of the institution, the reformers would simply identify and agree upon certain problem areas in which Congress was failing to fulfill the tasks set for it.
3. Then the best of the proposed remedies to the problems could be selected and enacted.

But however attractive such an orderly reformation might be, its preconditions—consensus on goals and precise calculations of means-ends relationships—are rarely realizable in real-world situations.[3] The major task of this study therefore will be to describe the political dimensions of congressional reform.

Discovering the Politics of Reform

Chapter 1. The most striking feature of congressional reformism is that those who write and speak on the subject have more than one "Congress" in mind. Theories of reform (if we can call them that) vary widely in the priority of the functions they assign to Congress. These theories spring from diverse policy orientations—and even from conflicting interpretations of democratic institutions in general. Thus, in Chapter 1, we discuss three alternative theories of congressional functions and specify the probable motivations and consequences of these theories.

---

[3] We are indebted to Charles E. Lindblom for his critique of the system of rational-comprehensive problem solving, although its application to congressional reform is our responsibility. See Lindblom's "The Science of 'Muddling Through,'" *Public Administration Review*, 19 (Spring 1959), 79–88; and his *The Intelligence of Democracy* (New York: Free Press of Glencoe, 1965), pp. 137–143.

Chapter 2. The claim that legislatures are suffering from, among other things, a badly tarnished "public image" is commonplace. Sometimes it is further contended that congressional reforms will be caused and conditioned by public attitudes. We are not satisfied with the relatively sparse data on public response to political institutions, but we will present some of the available material in Chapter 2. Our conclusions on the nature of the public assessment of Congress are necessarily tentative, but we think they should be of interest to students of public opinion as well as students of legislative institutions.

Chapters 3 and 4. Ultimately, of course, the decisions concerning congressional structures and practices must be made by Representatives and Senators themselves. Observers too frequently reach conclusions without sufficient sensitivity to the actual problems that Representatives and Senators face. Determined not to emulate Woodrow Wilson—who wrote his celebrated book *Congressional Government* without visiting Capitol Hill—we decided to probe, in as sophisticated a fashion as we knew, the attitudes of Congressmen themselves toward institutional change. Accordingly, during 1963 and 1964 we interviewed a sample of 118 members of the House of Representatives. (The methodology of our survey is explained in detail in Appendix A.) We asked the Representatives to describe their jobs, to outline the functions they thought Congress should perform, and to discuss the problems they encountered in fulfilling their objectives. Our respondents were also asked to react to a number of specific reform proposals, which have been put forward by journalists, scholars, Congressmen, and other observers. Some of the findings of this survey—and the implications of these findings for the future of Congress—are reported in Chapters 3 and 4 and in Appendix B.

Congressmen vary widely in their personal goals and institutional objectives, in their satisfaction with their jobs, and in their assessments of the problems of the legislative body. We attempt to relate these divergent attitudes to such variable factors as types of constituencies, general voting records, and seniority. Also, by analyzing the attitudes of these legislators toward reform proposals, we are able to identify and characterize the "reform" and "anti-reform" Congressmen and to set forth in Chapters 3 and 4 a reasonably precise specification of the conditions that both stimulate and inhibit innovation in congressional procedures.

Chapter 5. Subsequent to our survey, the 89th Congress convened in Washington to compile a legislative record unique in modern times. Driven by unusually large partisan majorities, Congress responded to President Johnson's leadership by enacting many of the "Great Society" programs. The unique partisan complexion of the two houses reflected itself in several structural and procedural changes, which illustrate our findings on the politics of reform. Some of these changes are reported in Chapter 5 in the form of a case study.

A Strategy of "Incremental Idealism"

Though our book is primarily empirical, we are not insensitive to the implications that our findings may have for innovative behavior. We presume that this study will serve as an antidote for much of the previous reformist literature, in which the authors accept little or no responsibility for the political implications of their arguments.

We are not unaware that the contemporary Congress has demonstrated serious deficiencies in meeting its responsibilities as a vital instrument of democratic government. These deficiencies are matters of legitimate concern, and one is justified in searching about for solutions. We will attempt to show why congressional innovation has failed to conform to the conventional notions about rational problem solving, and we will discuss whether rational planning is foreclosed as a technique for dealing with these problems.

Rational problem solving and incrementalism—the competing methodologies of large-scale change and of small, gradual additions arising from the reduction of dissension—usually form the fulcrums on which the issues of congressional reform are weighed. In debates on reform, rationalists and pragmatists often talk past one another, becoming conscientious objectors to each other's contrasting visions of the future. The rationalists state their case in terms of long-range, comprehensive developments and needs. They often fail to consider how to move from what is possible today to what seems necessary tomorrow. The pragmatists tend to cast their analyses of Congress in the light of current political feasibility. This pragmatic attitude leads to an intellectual dead end; for knowledge of what is needed should be based on an understanding of the problem and not merely on political feasibility.

What these debates over the future of Congress have typically lacked is a middle ground, which bridges the long-term potential of the institution with the pragmatic sense of what is attainable in the short term. Political scientists are in serious need of a new strategy of "incremental idealism," which combines a vision of the future with practical techniques for change in· an ongoing institution.[4] We have thought it appropriate merely to suggest the outlines that such a strategy might take. We believe that our study will provide a foundation on which others may build.

[4] For a discussion of applied middle-range social analysis, see S. M. Miller, "Prospects: The Applied Sociology of the Center-City," in *Applied Sociology*, eds. Alvin W. Gouldner and S. M. Miller (New York: Free Press of Glencoe, 1965), pp. 441–456.

1 PATHWAYS TO REFORM

Scholars are accustomed to saying that politics involves the conflict over the distribution of society's material and symbolic resources by official institutions.[1] With each edition of the daily newspapers, citizens are reminded of the seemingly unending contests for advantage in the allocation of these resources. Frequently, these contests appear to be blatant struggles for material advantage, such as those between labor and management, between producers and their competitors, or between producers and consumers. Sometimes, the conflicts seem to be over such symbolic values as status, patriotism, religion, morality, or ideology. But perhaps most often, the struggles are waged over both material and symbolic values, as in civil rights, federal-state relations, urban-rural issues, and many aspects of foreign policy. In these struggles, the involvement of symbolic values should not be dismissed as the mere waving of semantic battle flags, for the outcomes profoundly affect the character of the American society and the nature of its political system.[2]

At a superficial glance, procedural issues may appear drab indeed in comparison with the colorful and well-documented struggles of material and symbolic interests. Yet the structures and procedures of public institutions profoundly influence and are influenced by the allocation of both material and symbolic resources in a society. Jus-

[1] This concept is a variant on the familiar definition offered in David Easton, *The Political System* (New York: Alfred A. Knopf, 1953), pp. 130ff.

[2] See Murray Edelman, *The Symbolic Uses of Politics* (Urbana: University of Illinois Press, 1964).

tice Felix Frankfurter's dictum on the importance of this relationship bears frequent repeating: "The history of American freedom is, in no small measure, the history of procedure."[3]

The power of any institution within a system directly affects those interests making demands on that institution as well as the many other interests whose demands are made at other power points in the system. Interests that see their objectives consistently promoted by Congress are necessarily interested spectators in the recurrent controversies over congressional prerogatives. In the same way, interests that look to the Presidency or the courts or the executive agencies as their defenders are apt to view congressional powers suspiciously.

Though not often articulated, the stakes in these contests are well understood by the participants. "In point of fact," writes Clinton Rossiter, "the struggle over the powers of the Presidency as against Congress . . . is only a secondary campaign in a political war over the future of America."[4] The organization and procedure of public institutions actually serve to structure the contests in which interests pursue their goals. Because "structural" issues so directly affect policy, it is hardly surprising that interested observers can simultaneously view Capitol Hill as either a "rubber stamp" or an "obstacle course."

One perceptive critic of Congress has suggested that so-called structural issues may be more "spiritual" than technical.[5] Witness, for example, the periodic and symptomatic controversies over such analogous structural problems as the decision-making powers of the Supreme Court or, more recently, the validity of alternative theories of representation—a debate precipitated by the Court's 1964 enunciation of the "one man, one vote" principle. Like the debates over the congressional role, these controversies partly involve the classic confrontation between the majoritarian democrats, who would create public institutions closely reflective of the popular will, and the modern-day exponents of John Calhoun's "concurrent majority," who believe that these same institutions

[3] *Malinski v. New York* 324 U.S. 401 (1945). The reference was to the rights of defendants in judicial proceedings.

[4] Clinton Rossiter, *The American Presidency* (New York: New American Library, 1956), pp. 150–151.

[5] David T. Bazelon, "Non-Rule in America," *Commentary*, 36 (December 1963), 439–440. See also Charles E. Lindblom, *The Intelligence of Democracy* (New York: Free Press of Glencoe, 1965), pp. 236–237.

should embody interests not readily calculable in terms of majoritarian mathematics. And, of course, in such a confrontation, a person's position is influenced by his opinions about the nature of man, the function of political institutions, and the priorities of competing public needs—all concerns of traditional normative political theory.

The issues of congressional structure therefore stand astride both the pragmatic and the philosophical aspects of American political life. Congressional reform is in a very real sense a bread-and-butter issue—whether or not the public readily perceives it as such. And the "spiritual" aspects of reformism are clear manifestations of familiar themes in American political thought.

"Parliaments, Go Home!"

The present dissatisfaction with legislative performance is ironic in view of the supreme place assigned to legislatures by classic democratic theory. Indeed, Parliament's claims against the ascendancy of the Crown occasioned the first skirmishes of the democratic revolution. Democratic theorists of the seventeenth and eighteenth centuries labored tenaciously to justify the legitimacy of the legislative power, described by John Locke as "that which has a right to direct how the force of the commonwealth shall be employed for preserving the community and the members of it."[6] Further, he insisted that the peculiarly intimate relationship of the representative assembly to the sovereign electorate rendered the legislature "not only the supreme power of the commonwealth, but sacred and unalterable in the hands where the community have once placed it."[7] It is hardly surprising that the Founding Fathers should devote Article I of the Constitution to the structure and powers of Congress.

Counterrevolutionary forces were already at work in the Constitutional Convention of 1787. Although the Framers were accustomed to viewing colonial legislatures as champions of the people against the power of the Crown-appointed governors, the more immediate experience of the Continental Congress and the Articles of Confederation vividly suggested that legislatures were unsuited

---

[6] John Locke, *Second Treatise on Civil Government* (London: J. M. Dent & Sons, 1924), p. 190.

[7] Locke, pp. 183–184.

for waging wars and conducting diplomacy.[8] James Madison argued that, in a republic, legislatures are more disposed to tyranny than are narrowly restrained executives; and he concluded that "the legislative department is everywhere extending the sphere of its activity and drawing all power into its impetuous vortex." The designers of the earlier state constitutions, he wrote, "seem never to have recollected the danger from legislative usurpations, which, by assembling all power in the same hands, must lead to the same tyranny as is threatened by executive usurpations."[9]

The ingenious solution of the Framers of the Constitution is familiar to every high school civics student: rather than "a mere demarcation on parchment" of the powers of the branches of government, these branches should be "so far connected and blended as to give to each a constitutional control over the others."[10] Thus, Article II contained a breathtaking array of executive prerogatives, which presented the Presidency with a potentially significant role in the legislative process.[11]

In the United States and Great Britain, the nineteenth century was an age of parliamentary ascendancy. One hundred years ago, Sir Henry Sumner Maine wrote: "The energy of legislatures is the prime characteristic of modern societies." The second great phase of the democratic revolution, the enfranchisement of the laboring masses, reinforced the legislative prerogatives which had been won in the earlier battles with the Crown. In the United States, the constitutional formula of blended powers worked reasonably well but resulted in alternating periods of executive and legislative hegemony. Following the Civil War, the phenomenon which Woodrow Wilson termed "congressional government" was accompanied by a prolonged eclipse of presidential powers. Wilson perhaps

[8] There was apparently little discussion in the Convention of the "grand design" of congressional powers. However, the working draft of the Constitution gave Congress the power to "make war." After a brief but fascinating exchange, it was determined to substitute "declare" for "make." See Arthur T. Prescott, *Drafting the Federal Constitution* (University, La.: Louisiana State University Press, 1941), pp. 513–514.

[9] *Federalist*, ed. Max Beloff (Oxford: Basil Blackwell, 1948), 48, p. 253.

[10] *Federalist*, 48, pp. 252, 256. For an analysis of the Madisonian solution to the problem of tyranny, see Robert A. Dahl, *A Preface to Democratic Theory* (Chicago: University of Chicago Press, 1956), Chap. 1.

[11] The leading source on the origins of the Presidency remains Charles C. Thach, *Creation of the Presidency, 1775–1789* (Baltimore: Johns Hopkins University Press, 1922).

exaggerated the actual situation, but his conclusion was at least expressive of the era: "Congress [is] the dominant, nay, the irresistible, power of the federal system, relegating some of the chief balances of the Constitution to an insignificant role . . ."[12]

Hardly any observer in the mid-twentieth century would describe legislatures in terms of "energy" or "irresistible power." The decline of parliaments, if not universally manifested, is at least universally commented upon. Students of British institutions note "a rapid trend towards the exaltation of the executive (both Cabinet ministers and civil servants) at the expense of the House of Commons."[13] Under the present system of rigid party loyalty, Commons has yielded the power of the Victorian Parliaments to overthrow a cabinet by cross-bench voting. Other parliamentary powers are severely atrophied. In the French Fourth Republic, the *immobilisme* of the ascendant National Assembly produced widespread public disillusionment and, ultimately, the takeover by antiparliament Gaullists in 1958. Leaders in the developing nations, sensing that they cannot indulge in the alleged inefficiencies and delays of what Indonesian President Sukarno called "free-fight liberalism," often shunt legislatures aside in favor of centralized administration or military rule. Stephen K. Bailey imagines that scrawled in invisible ink on the walls of the empty parliament buildings are the words "Parliaments, go home!"[14]

Has Congress Declined ?

The American Congress has demonstrated remarkably keen instincts for survival in this age of executive ascendancy. Congressmen and Senators are fond of repeating that Congress is the most powerful legislature anywhere in the world. They are probably right; indeed, it would be incorrect to say that congressional powers have declined in any absolute sense. The twentieth-century Congress involves itself with a host of governmental programs that, in the nineteenth century, were performed by local or private entities,

---

[12] Woodrow Wilson, *Congressional Government* (New York: Meridian Books, 1955), p. 23.

[13] "House in Decline," *The Economist* (August 20, 1960), p. 705.

[14] Stephen K. Bailey, "Is Congress the Old Frontier?" in *Continuing Crisis in American Politics,* ed. Marian D. Irish (Englewood Cliffs, N.J.: Prentice-Hall, 1963), p. 69.

or not at all. The Clays, Calhouns, and Websters could devote a
generation or more to refining the few great controversies of the
Republic; the contemporary legislator, on the other hand, finds
himself daily beset by a staggering number and variety of public
issues.

The crude indicators in Table 1.1 are symptomatic of the
increasing congressional work load: the volume of public legislation

TABLE 1.1

Two Indicators of the Congressional Workload

Congress	Public laws passed	Days in session
1st (1789–91)	108	519
49th (1885–87)	424	330
56th (1899–1901)	443	277
62nd (1911–13)	530	500
69th (1925–27)	808	297
77th (1941–42)	850	711
85th (1957–58)	936	469
87th (1961–62)	885	545

Source: Final edition, House Calendars. See also U.S. House
of Representatives, Committee on Administration, *History of
the United States House of Representatives*, by George B. Galloway (Washington, 1961), pp. 108–109.

has increased; and the length of sessions, formerly quite variable,
has apparently stabilized to embrace virtually a 12-month schedule.
Also, the growing size, complexity, educational level, and mass-media
exposure of constituencies have greatly increased the volume of
communications handled by congressional offices. The quantity and
the diversity of legislative business create frustrations for Congress, to be sure; and it is open to question whether congressional
involvement in governing is as meaningful as it once was. But the
fact of this involvement itself can hardly be questioned. There has
been no absolute decline of congressional functions.

The position of Congress relative to the executive is quite another
matter, and on this point there is virtual consensus that the high-
water mark of legislative influence has passed. Few would dissent
from the judgment of Edward S. Corwin that "Taken by and
large, the history of the Presidency is a history of aggrandize-

ment . . .''[15] This ''aggrandizement'' is most noticeable in the initiation of legislative proposals. Two generations ago, Henry Lee McBain observed that the President had emerged as ''Chief Legislator''; now, ''the President's program'' is institutionalized as a point of departure for the legislative process.[16] Presidential initiation of legislation has made two critical inroads on the influence of Congress. First, the important function of setting the agenda has largely been passed on by Congress to the President and his staff. Second, the contestants in political struggles increasingly tend to press their claims and resolve their differences through the agencies ''downtown'' rather than in the halls of Congress. The processes of representation and conciliation may be largely effected even before Congress receives the executive proposals.

Against this background of executive dominance, critics of every political persuasion have found Congress relegated to a secondary level of power. The assessment by George B. Galloway, written on the eve of the Legislative Reorganization Act of 1946, would still be accepted by most observers:

> Overworked and underpaid, often lampooned by the press and unfairly criticized by the thoughtless, our national legislature had fallen from its once high estate. Few any longer regarded it as the keystone of the federal arch. With Congress overwhelmed by its great responsibilities, operating under its ancient ritual, the streamlined age . . . seemed to have passed it by.[17]

None are more sensitive to this ebbing of power than the legislators themselves. ''Every day in every way the power of the Congress is being diluted,'' a veteran Congressman recently lamented.[18] The findings reported in Chapter 3 show this lament to be a prevalent mood on Capitol Hill.

[15] Edward S. Corwin, *The President, Office and Powers*, 4th ed. (New York: New York University Press, 1957), pp. 29–30.

[16] See Richard Neustadt's two articles, ''Presidency and Legislation: The Growth of Central Clearance,'' *American Political Science Review*, 48 (September 1954), 641–671, and ''Presidency and Legislation: Planning the President's Program,'' *ibid.*, 49 (December 1955), 998–1021.

[17] George B. Galloway, *Congress at the Crossroads* (New York: Thomas Y. Crowell, 1946), pp. 5–6.

[18] F. Edward Hébert (D-La.), *The Congress and America's Future*, Report of the Seventh Air Force Academy Assembly (Colorado Springs: U.S. Air Force Academy, 1965), p. 22.

The reasons for Congress' relative decline are diverse. Many of the factors in the decline of congressional power are by-products of the vastly changed environment in which Congress must operate. Since World War II, foreign and military affairs have assumed an unprecedented dominance in public discussions and federal expenditures. Presidential initiative in these areas is enunciated in the Constitution and validated by historical experience; and, since these international and military concerns are enhanced by current events, the President and the executive establishment are in turn enhanced.[19] The continuous semicrises of our age have welded the President's powers as Commander-in-Chief and his prerogatives as "the sole organ of the nation in foreign affairs."

A related factor in the decline of the power of Congress is the increasing diversity and complexity of policy problems. The information required for governmental decision making is enormously complicated. Congress has wrestled manfully with this problem, but it struggles under an inherent disadvantage—the executive bureaucracy with its 2.5 million skilled and knowledgeable employees. By establishing a semipermanent professional staff and by exploiting the standing-committee system for area specialization, Congress has succeeded in blunting the effects of these inherent executive advantages. These and other stratagems will insure the survival of Congress as an institution; but whether the changes will be sufficient to preserve congressional vitality (or regain it, depending upon one's viewpoint) is another question altogether.

The past two decades have not been void of institutional innovation on Capitol Hill. The landmark Legislative Reorganization Act of 1946, which followed extensive investigations by the Joint Committee chaired by Senator Robert M. LaFollette, Jr., and then-Representative A. S. Mike Monroney, produced far-reaching changes in congressional operations—especially with increased staffing and with reduction of the number of standing committees.[20] Dissatisfaction with the House Rules Committee's successful block-

---

[19] On this general question, see the discussion by Richard Neustadt in *The Congress and America's Future*, ed. David B. Truman (Englewood Cliffs, N.J.: Prentice-Hall, 1965), pp. 109–112.

[20] An evaluation of the 1946 Act is found in George B. Galloway, *Congressional Reorganization Revisited* (College Park, Md.: University of Maryland Bureau of Governmental Research, 1956). For a discussion of omnibus appropriations and the "legislative budget," see John S. Saloma, *The Responsible Use of Power* (Washington: American Enterprise Institute, 1964).

ade of liberal legislation led to enactment of the ''21-day rule'' device in 1949–1951, and again in 1965, and to an enlargement of the committee in 1961.[21] In the Senate, several marginal rules changes were enacted in 1963; and concern over the Senate's reputation in the aftermath of the Bobby Baker scandals led in 1964–1965 to the reexamination of the rules and the appointment of a Committee on Ethics. In addition, numerous minor innovations since World War II have accompanied the increasing congressional work load. In view of the apparent conservatism of the congressional power structure, these innovations are surprising in their frequency, if not in the scope of their results.

Most reform-minded observers and Congressmen consider these recent changes inadequate and prescribe more drastic medicine. In the face of what they have diagnosed as a severe case of ''standpatism,'' reformers have persisted in their bombardment of the reluctant patient with all manner of nostrums. No less than 426 separate proposals were gathered during 41 days of hearings in 1965.[22] An elucidation of the most prevalent of the various strains of reformism is best accomplished through a description of the premises which underlie these reform proposals.

Theories of Congress

The Congress that emerged from the Philadelphia Convention of 1787 was the outgrowth of a prolonged institutional struggle, which affected both sides of the Atlantic and which produced a rather explicit theory of legislative functions. Though scholars often correctly observe that the Founding Fathers were pragmatic politicians who were loath to bind succeeding generations to excessively rigid formulations, they tend to neglect the fact that the pragmatism of the Framers was conditioned by an accepted body of political thought—a set of explicit beliefs about the nature of man and his institutions that were assumed to be valid. The Framers were not always able to see what they had done, but a serious study of their debates and commentaries indicates that they were intensely aware of what it was they *intended* to do.

[21] Chapter 5 recounts the history of the 1965 innovations.

[22] U.S. Congress, Joint Committee on the Organization of the Congress, *Second Interim Report* (Senate Report 948, 89th Congress, 2nd Session, 1966), pp. 11–29.

Nothing less should be asked of contemporary students of
legislative institutions. The advice which Harold D. Smith, then
director of the Budget Bureau, gave to the LaFollette-Monroney
Committee in 1945 is so relevant that it deserves repeating:

> This is a different sort of world from that which existed when
> the Constitutional Convention devised the framework of our
> government. Yet we still lack a penetrating and practical restate-
> ment of the role of representative assemblies in light of the chang-
> ing problems under which they operate. . . . Your own talents
> and the keenest minds you can command could very well be
> devoted to rethinking the functions of the Congress under present
> conditions. A sound reformulation of the role of the representa-
> tive body is basic to all the work of your committee.[23]

This was and is sound intellectual procedure, quite apart from the
question of whether the constitutional formula demands radical
revision. More important, Smith's injunction has not always been
heeded by the proponents of congressional reform, including the
LaFollette-Monroney Committee itself.

In recent years, a number of students have devoted explicit
attention to the functions that the contemporary Congress performs
in the political system.[24] Sometimes their conclusions have led them
to propose or to evaluate remedial steps that would alter the roles of
Congress or would assist it in performing its present roles more
effectively. But it is fair to conclude that, by and large, students
of Congress have not been sufficiently attentive to the theory of
Congress. Ralph K. Huitt observed that "there is no 'model' of a
proper legislature to which men of good intention can repair."[25]

What should be included in a theory of the legislature? Such a
theory would begin with a series of factual generalizations specify-
ing those functions that the legislature does in fact perform in a
political system. Within this framework, specific traditions and
practices may be accounted for and their consequences (intended or

[23] U.S. Congress, Joint Committee on the Organization of the Congress,
Hearings, Part 3 (Washington: Government Printing Office, 1945), pp. 670–671.

[24] Two useful examples are Aaron Wildavsky, *The Politics of the Budgetary
Process* (Boston: Little, Brown & Co., 1964); and Samuel Huntington, *The
Common Defense* (New York: Columbia University Press, 1961), esp. pp.
123–146.

[25] Ralph K. Huitt, "What Can We Do About Congress?" *Milwaukee
Journal,* Part 5 (December 13, 1964), p. 1.

not) for the system may be spelled out. The analyst who chooses not to lay down his tools at this point would then set forth his view of an ideal legislature in an ideal system. He would specify the points of disharmony between this ideal world and the real world. Finally, he would propose specific innovations that would bring the ideal world into being.

Hopefully, the theorist would be attentive to the probable and the unintended consequences of these innovations. More attention to objectives and possible consequences would make the proposal of reforms more meaningful than it has been in the past.[26]

Implicit in most of the recent writing on congressional reform are concepts that can be categorized into reasonably distinct theories of the proper functions of a legislative body. These theories are three in number: the "literary" theory, based primarily on a literal reading of the Constitution; the "executive-force" theory, which stresses policy leadership emanating from the President and the bureaucracy; and the "party-government" theory, which emphasizes the legislature's responsibility to the national party constituency. In terms of the weight given Congress in relation to the executive, the literary theory comes closest to legislative supremacy, the executive-force theory stands at the opposite pole, and the party-government theory stands somewhere in between. The overall weight that each theory gives to Congress is less important, however, than the kinds of functions which each assigns to Congress and to the other branches of government.

THE LITERARY THEORY

The literary theory is essentially a restatement of the constitutional formulation of blended and coordinate powers—the "institutionalized mutual responsibility of coequals."[27] Adherence to this position need not imply a naive belief that nothing fundamental in the congressional environment has changed since 1789; it does imply, however, that the constitutional delineation of functions is still valid and that the relative weight assigned to the three

[26] See Ralph K. Huitt, "Congressional Reorganization: The Next Chapter," (a paper presented at the annual meeting of the American Political Science Association, Chicago, Illinois, September 8–12, 1964).

[27] Ernest S. Griffith, *Congress: Its Contemporary Role* (New York: New York University Press, 1951), p. 7.

branches by the Constitution is essentially correct. Proponents of
this point of view maintain that Congress should exercise *at least*
its present level of power within the political system.

Reversing the flow of events. Advocates of the literary theory
are most commonly obsessed with what they interpret as a severe,
and perhaps fatal, erosion of congressional prerogatives. James
Burnham, whose book *Congress and the American Tradition* is a
fascinating and incisive polemic, sounded the theme when he
declared:

> What the American government system now needs is . . . a
> very considerably strengthened Congress: strengthened in the
> political sense of gaining (regaining, in historical fact) increased
> relative weight within the political equilibrium. On this assump-
> tion . . . the performance of Congress will be judged much less
> than stellar.[28]

The decline and fall of Congress, according to this theory, can be
attributed to three developments. Most fundamental of these
developments is the advent of the sprawling welfare state, which
makes the executive branch the source of many governmental
services now largely beyond legislative control. Secondly, the
compelling public image of the strong President and the academic
and journalistic criticisms of legislative institutions reduce public
support for Congress. Finally, Congress itself abets its declining
influence by "failing to fight back stoutly and intelligently" and
by dissipating its resistance to encroachments in "verbal complaints and rhetorical grumblings, which fizzle out in petty amendments of administration projects. Congress has been shadow-box-
ing, not fighting."[29] This theme is often heard from legislators
themselves and is reminiscent of former Congressman Dewey
Short's (R-Mo.) indictment of the House of Representatives as
"that supine, subservient, soporific, supercilious, pusillanimous
body of nitwits." Many literary-theory advocates insist that these
trends toward executive empire building and judicial activism
could be reversed if Congressmen would only "stiffen their spines"
against unconstitutional intrusions upon their legislative powers.

At least one literary theorist does not share this pessimism over

[28] James Burnham, *Congress and the American Tradition* (Chicago: Henry
Regnery, 1959), p. 276.
[29] Burnham, pp. 277–278.

legislative decline. In fact, argues Willmoore Kendall, Congress wins more frequently than is generally supposed in its tug-of-war with the executive. For one thing, many congressional victories are hidden from public view: President Franklin D. Roosevelt obtained the highly publicized Tennessee Valley Authority, for example, but what ever happened to proposals for a spate of TVA's in other river basins? Second, no one can ever know how many proposals the executive refrains from making because of expected congressional resistance—"the ten thousand . . . drastic proposals cooking away in ten thousand bureaucratic heads in Washington that the attackers [of tradition] do not dare even to embody in a bill, do not dare even to mention, because the proposals would not stand a Chinaman's chance." Thus, Kendall enjoins the supporters of Congress to keep up their courage "if they are going to keep on winning."[30]

The "republican force." Advocates of the literary theory predictably perceive that their values and interests are disadvantaged by the policies of the executive and the judiciary, and they look upon revitalization of Congress as the means of reweighting the balance in their favor. This pro-Congress contingent is a not inconsiderable group, which looks to Capitol Hill for the reversal of the long-term trends of centralism and paternalism. This "republican force," as Alfred de Grazia has termed it, has gathered many recruits during the past generation: economic conservatives, who are hostile to post-New Deal social-welfare legislation; advocates of "states' rights," who find local autonomy threatened on every front by the courts and the executive; fundamentalists, who are confused and dismayed by modernism and secularism; and "the rural folk"—rural and small-town interests who feel themselves being plowed under by the alien trends of urbanism. All of these groups demand that Congress be preserved as a check upon the hostile powers entrenched elsewhere in the governmental system.

Although the contemporary Supreme Court is consistently criticized for usurping the legislative function, the President and his executive establishment are seen as the greatest enemies of the republican virtues. As the president of the Americans for Constitutional Action told the Joint Committee on the Organization of the Congress in June 1965:

[30] Willmoore Kendall, *The Conservative Affirmation* (Chicago: Henry Regnery, 1963), pp. 15, 30–31, 85.

The President is the head of the party. He exercises vast powers in spending the money appropriated by Congress. He represents the father image in the paternalistic order of government. He represents the dominant political philosophy. All the resources of the political party and of socialist-oriented intellectuals are committed to the increase of his powers and to the destruction of the constitutional restraints.[31]

Such critics insist that supporters of a strong Presidency identify Congress as the "obstacle course" to their goals. "As Congress is the bulwark of that [constitutional] system, the goal of the socialist planners is to be won by rendering Congress ineffectual."[32]

Representatives and Senators have reasons quite apart from ideology for resisting the attrition of their powers and their influence. Many express the understandable frustration of men in high public office who find that their actual influence is not what they expected it would be. Thus, Senator Abraham Ribicoff (D-Conn.), certainly no friend of the policy positions of most literary theorists, complained bitterly in 1964 that Congress has "surrendered its rightful leadership in the law-making process to the White House." The legislative branch, he wrote, "now merely filters legislative proposals from the President . . . These days no one expects Congress to devise important bills. Instead, the legislative views of the President dominate the press, the public, and Congress itself."[33] This frustration is not uncommon among legislators, regardless of their political affiliation.

Tenets of the theory. According to the advocates of the literary theory, Congress must assert its right to exercise "all legislative powers." Policies should be initiated by Congress at least as often as by the executive, for "the primary business of the legislature in a democratic republic is to answer the big questions of policy."[34] Executive officials would be consulted on technical aspects of policy making, but they should be prohibited from lobbying or pressuring. When the executive, by necessity, initiates legislative proposals, it

[31] Maj. Gen. Thomas A. Lane (USA, Ret.), in U.S. Congress, Joint Committee on the Organization of the Congress, *Hearings,* Part 7 (Washington: Government Printing Office, 1965), p. 1090. Referred to hereafter as *Joint Committee Hearings* (1965).

[32] Lane, *Joint Committee Hearings* (1965).

[33] *Saturday Evening Post* (March 21, 1964), p. 10. See also the remarks of Senator Clark in *Joint Committee Hearings,* Part 1 (1965), pp. 18–19.

[34] Burnham, p. 349.

should do so in an advisory capacity, fully respectful of congressional supremacy in lawmaking. The ultimate authority of elected laymen to set priorities on complicated and technical matters is an indispensible feature of democratic government.

For the defender of the literary theory, the legislator's legitimacy as the ultimate policy maker rests on his near-monopoly of the channels of communication to the sovereign electorate. Since the President also is elected by and responsible to the electorate, this monopoly is not total. But the President is the only elected official in the executive branch; his constituency is diffuse, his mandate imprecise. Congressmen, on the other hand, are specific and precise representatives, who "necessarily and properly reflect the attitudes and needs of their individual districts."[35] The legislative process, therefore, is not a simple "yes" or "no" vote on policy alternatives but a complex combinatorial process through which numerous and shifting minority claims are acknowledged. One contemporary scholar has defended the particularity of congressional representation in the following manner:

> Congress has the strength of the free enterprise system; it multiplies the decision-makers, the points of access to influence and power, and the creative moving agents. It is hard to believe that a small group of leaders could do better. What would be gained in orderliness might well be lost in vitality and in sensitiveness to the pressures for change. Moreover, Congress resembles the social system it serves; it reflects the diversity of the country. There is much to be said for a system in which almost every interest can find some spokesman, in which every cause can strike a blow, however feeble, in its own behalf.[36]

More often than not, in a government modeled on the literary theory, no legislative decision can be reached on momentous political conflicts: on intensely felt issues at least, a government that acts before a "concurrent majority" can be found or constructed is tyrannical.[37] Thorough exploration of the consensus of

[35] Griffith, p. 3. See also Kendall, pp. 41ff.

[36] Ralph K. Huitt, "Congressional Organization in the Field of Money and Credit" in Commission on Money and Credit, *Fiscal and Debt Management Policies* (Englewood Cliffs, N.J.: Prentice-Hall, 1963), p. 494. For a discussion of the "defensive advantages" that minorities exercise in the congressional system, see David B. Truman, *The Governmental Process* (New York: Alfred A. Knopf, 1951), Chaps. 11 and 12.

[37] See the discussion of numerical and concurrent majorities in Burnham, Chaps. 24–25.

the society is the high function of the elected policy maker and the essence of the "legislative way of life." Neither speed, efficiency, nor "passing a lot of laws" are valid indicators of congressional effectiveness in performing these delicate deliberative tasks. From a conservative vantage point, in fact, the refusal to pass laws is often a blessing.

All advocates of the literary theory view executive power with suspicion, but they differ on the extent to which they think the executive should be cut down. The theory requires merely a semblance of balance among the branches of government; and constitutional history provides ample precedents for a strong and autonomous executive, as well as an activist Congress. However, one version of the literary theory—which we call the "Whig" variant —would enthrone Congress as *the* dominant institution in the political system. This variant of the theory would reduce Presidents to weaklings, even in foreign and military affairs.[38] The degree to which one wishes to pare down executive power is presumably related to the depth of one's dissatisfaction with contemporary political trends.

On this much the literary theory is clear: what Congress proposes, the executive should dispose. The executive branch should engage in the detailed implementation of laws that are as specific and detailed as possible, leaving bureaucrats little leeway for interpretation. Curiously, one advocate of the literary theory, Burnham, takes an opposite view. The bureaucracy, which conducts the day-to-day operations of government, will always be able to circumvent detailed provisos laid down by Congress. Thus he reasons:

> . . . the only way to control the chief officials of the colossal managerial-bureaucratic state is to give an unambiguous main policy directive, to define clear limits, and then to insist on strict public accountability for satisfactory performance. . . .
> If the reins are kept too tight, the horse will get the bit in its teeth. They must normally be loose, if the curbing is to be effec-

---

[38] In a forthcoming analysis, John S. Saloma distinguishes between "Presidential-Constitutionalists" and "Whigs," the latter of whom advocate strong congressional leadership and weak executives. See his "Congressional Performance: Evaluation and Implications for Reform" (in preparation). For an analysis that is vintage Whiggism, see Alfred de Grazia's *Republic in Crisis* (New York: Federal Legal Press, 1965).

tive. If Congress tries to watch each million, the billions will get away.[39]

In any event, Congress must exercise extensive supervision (usually termed "oversight") of the administration of laws, intervening vigorously and often to ensure compliance. And, if necessary, remedial legislation should be passed.

The courts, in this view, should similarly be prevented from usurping legislative functions. The jurists should recognize that a wide variety of "political questions" are the proper sphere of only the elected decision makers. In the opinion of the "constitutionalists," the judicial "lawmaking" that most impinges upon legislative autonomy is the apportionment ruling.[40] They argue, first, that electoral laws are by nature political questions which should be determined by the elected bodies themselves. Secondly, the Court's newly enunciated "one man, one vote" criterion will clearly dilute the influence of the rural minority, thus rendering the collective congressional constituency more nearly like that of the President. This melding of constituencies, in the judgment of constitutionalists, will reduce the healthy dichotomy of the two branches of government. And in political terms, it will submerge those constituencies that have traditionally been championed by Congress but not by the executive.[41]

The other major area of judicial impingement upon Congress is the Court's review of alleged violations of civil liberties that result from legislative investigations.[42] While others might argue that the Court's involvement in such questions has been marginal and discontinuous, the constitutionalist interprets such forays as a trespass upon Congress' control over its own rules and procedures.

[39] Burnham, p. 350.

[40] *Wesberry v. Sanders* 376 U.S. 1 (1964). In the wake of this decision, House Judiciary Committee Chairman Emanuel Celler (D-N.Y.) sponsored a bill (H.R. 5505) during the 89th Congress that would require congressional districts to deviate no more than 15 percent (greater or less) from the average size in a given state. The bill also specifies that districts be of "contiguous territory, in as compact form as practicable." The House passed the measure; but, as of this writing, the Senate had not acted upon it.

[41] See Andrew Hacker, "The Voice of 90 Million Americans," *New York Times Magazine* (March 4, 1962).

[42] See Martin Shapiro, *Law and Politics on the Supreme Court* (New York: Free Press of Glencoe, 1964), pp. 50–75.

Reform propositions. While there may be differences of opinion on precise means-ends relationships, the following list of reform propositions would probably be approved by most advocates of the literary theory:

A. Constituencies and the electoral system:
  1. Rather than rigid adherence to the "one man, one vote" principle, legislative apportionment should recognize the validity of other criteria of representation—geographic interests, for example, or political subdivisions—in order to ensure that the greatest possible diversity of interests is embodied in Congress.
  2. Congress itself—probably in concert with state and local authorities—should exercise authority over whatever electoral devices are employed.
  3. The electorate should be educated on congressional government through the initiation of public relations campaigns and the provision of more time for legislators in their districts.
B. Political parties:
  1. Innovations that would centralize the party under noncongressional control (for example, through national party councils) should be resisted.
  2. Diversified, rather than "responsible," party structure should be encouraged to stress the party function of building a national consensus.[43]
C. The Presidency:
  1. The 22nd Amendment, which limits the President to two terms, should be maintained.
  2. The presidential discretion in implementing policies and in withholding information from Congress should be limited.
  3. Presidential messages should be answered by formal speeches from congressional leaders, both majority and minority.
  4. The proposal that plans initiated by the President become effective unless vetoed by Congress should be opposed.

---

[43] Some ideologues (from both right and left) have urged a polarization of our two parties into a Liberal and a Conservative Party. Such a development would most probably be dysfunctional for conservatives favoring the literary theory of Congress since polarization would reduce the legislative "braking" function of dispersed, decentralized parties.

D. Congressional procedures:

   1. Staffs for individual legislators and committees should be moderately increased, with maximum staff assistance for minority members—perhaps even in reverse ratio to the size of the minority representation in Congress.

   2. Attempts to centralize congressional leadership should be resisted in order to maximize the deliberative and even obstructionist tendencies of the individual legislators.[44]

   3. Moderate dilatory devices, such as the Senate filibuster and a strong House Rules Committee, should be sanctioned.

   4. Legislators should continue to help constituents in dealing with the executive bureaucracy (so-called "casework").

   5. Congressional oversight of the executive should be facilitated through increased use of the General Accounting Office, of budgetary controls, of special investigative subcommittees, and of detailed committee review of legislation, appointments, and appropriations.

   6. Congress should resist formal ties to the executive through joint legislative-executive councils and should avoid dependence upon executive agencies for such commodities as travel or research facilities.

THE EXECUTIVE-FORCE THEORY

In a sense, the executive-force theory reverses the formulation of the literary theory: the executive initiates and implements; the legislature modifies and ratifies.

Which way is history going? The rationales for the executive-force theory illustrate the ambiguities of historical interpretation. Advocates of this theory either (a) concur with the constitutionalists' thesis that the balance of power has shifted radically toward the executive branch but propose that reforms should be instituted to ensure this new executive hegemony or (b) disagree entirely with that assessment and hold that legislative intimidation of executives is now more extreme than ever before. In either case, the conclusion is that the executive establishment ought to be

[44] A dissenter here is Samuel P. Huntington, who argues that centralized congressional leadership would revivify Congress. For reasons that will become apparent in the following sections, this development might actually have the opposite effect. See Huntington, "Congressional Responses to the Twentieth Century," in *The Congress and America's Future*, ed. David B. Truman.

granted wide latitude for decision making and substantial insula-
tion from legislative obstruction.

Adherents of the first rationale—the shift of the balance of
power toward the executive—cite historical precedents to show that
presidential ascendancy is a fulfillment of original constitutional
principles. Indeed, they hold that the ponderous counterbalances
devised by the Founding Fathers are viable only when supple-
mented by an initiator-ratifier relationship between the White
House and Capitol Hill.

The architects of the Presidency at the Constitutional Convention—Alexander Hamilton, James Wilson, and Gouverneur Morris
—were advocates of strong and vigorous executive responsibility.
Hamilton praised "energy" as the outstanding feature of good
government and declared that all men of good sense must agree on
the necessity of an energetic executive.[45] Federalist political theory
showed a decided preference for the executive partly because of its
distrust of the people. As Leonard White has characterized the
Federalist position, "Decisions on programs thought out by [well-
educated and cultivated] national leaders might be subject to the
vote of popular assemblies, but the latter . . . had neither the
capacity, nor the unity, to work out the plans themselves."[46]

The precedents established by the strong Presidents lend historical weight to this argument. Referring to Thomas Jefferson's active
intervention in legislation, Congressman Richard Bolling explains
that the early House of Representatives was "the organ of
ratification of the decisions presented to it by those members . . .
who . . . sat as agents of the President and his advisors."[47] The
demands of a national emergency—prompt, concerted action and
clarity of policy—have repeatedly strengthened the executive
branch. Looking back on the remarkable performance of the first
New Deal Congress, Franklin Roosevelt observed: "The letter of

[45] *Federalist*, 70.

[46] Leonard D. White, *The Federalists* (New York: Macmillan, 1956), p. 510.
"Statist" methods and democratic objectives find their convergence in
Herbert Croly, *The Promise of American Life*, ed. Arthur M. Schlesinger, Jr.
(Cambridge: Harvard University Press, 1965).

[47] Richard Bolling, *House out of Order* (New York: E. P. Dutton & Co.,
1965), p. 27. On the Jeffersonian strategy, see James M. Burns, *The Deadlock
of Democracy* (Englewood Cliffs, N.J.: Prentice-Hall, 1963), Chap. 2. A
thorough historical review is provided in Wilfred Binkley, *The President and
Congress* (New York: Alfred A. Knopf, 1947).

the Constitution wisely declared a separation, but the impulse of common purpose declares a union.''[48]

The present age of permanent semicrisis has reinforced this historical tendency because every contemporary President is required to be strong. The pull of executive leadership is thus seen as inevitable and irreversible. ''The cause of the opponents of a strong Presidency,'' Rossiter writes with finality, ''is ill-starred because they cannot win a war against American history. The strong Presidency is the product of events that cannot be undone and of forces that continue to roll.''[49]

The theory of the President-as-Chief-Legislator would appear to be an abstraction of things as they are. But some critics, not so sanguine about the course of recent events, still see the cards stacked in favor of the legislature; they believe the legislative branch more meddlesome than ever. Columnist Walter Lippmann, often called Washington's ''philosopher-in-residence,'' paints a bleak picture of executives cowering before the rampant power of legislatures. When the New Frontier program ran into legislative deadlock in 1963, he questioned, ''What kind of legislative body is it that will not or cannot legislate?'' And writing on the Fourth of July that year, he voiced his fears for the future of representative government:

> I find myself thinking how rarely free governments have been overthrown by foreign tyrants, except temporarily in time of war, but how often free governments have fallen because of their own weakness and incapacity. To one thinking such thoughts there is nothing reassuring about the present Congress.[50]

In Lippmann's opinion, ''derangement''of powers has occurred at the governmental level because representative assemblies, supported by mass opinion, have acquired ''the monopoly of effective powers.'' The ''enfeebled'' executive can no longer act decisively or rationally to solve complex public problems.[51]

A somewhat less cataclysmic interpretation of the ''deadlock of

---

[48] Cited in Corwin, p. 272.

[49] Rossiter, p. 151. See also Richard Neustadt, *Presidential Power: The Politics of Leadership* (New York: John Wiley, 1960).

[50] ''Strength to Govern Well,'' *Washington Post* (July 4, 1963), p. A 19.

[51] Walter Lippmann, *The Public Philosophy* (Boston: Little, Brown & Co., 1954), pp. 54–57.

democracy" is given by James M. Burns in his highly publicized critique of the Madisonian system of mutual distrust and irresponsibility. Entrenched on Capitol Hill by gerrymandered districts and the seniority system, legislators from stagnant, one-party regions are able to thwart liberal, urban majorities that represent the "presidential wings" of the two parties.[52]

From their vantage point at the western reaches of Pennsylvania Avenue, Presidents themselves are fervent believers in the power of Congress to frustrate their programs. In his television report of December 1962, President Kennedy admitted with a note of irony that "the fact is . . . that the Congress looks more powerful sitting here than it did when I was there in the Congress."[53]

The President's constituency. The legitimacy of executive dominance rests on a concept of representation quite at variance with the Madison-Calhoun pluralism of the literary theorists. As the only official elected by the whole population, the President is considered the embodiment of the nation. Legislators represent partial and minority interests; the President represents the "general will" of the community. Burns has given a more precise definition of this dichotomy:

> The Madisonian system finds its tension in the competition among struggling groups, multiparty factions, and mutually checking branches of government. The Jeffersonian system, a more hierarchical arrangement, finds its tension in the relation of leader and led, with the leader usually pressing his troops, like an army commander, and the troops usually restraining, but sometimes outrunning, their leader.[54]

Thus, Theodore Roosevelt saw the President as a "steward of the people"; and, some years before his own elevation to the office, Woodrow Wilson sensed its representative potentialities. "His is the only national voice in affairs," he declared in his 1907 Columbia

---

[52] The case is put in two of Burns' books, *Congress on Trial* (New York: Harper & Brothers, 1949), and *Deadlock of Democracy* (Englewood Cliffs, N.J.: Prentice-Hall, 1963).

[53] December 17, 1962. Reprinted in *Congressional Quarterly Weekly Report* (December 21, 1962), p. 2278.

[54] Burns, *Deadlock*, p. 337. For a remarkably similar analysis, see Burnham, p. 327.

University lectures. "He is the representative of no constituency, but of the whole people."[55]

The electoral rationale for executive dominance has obvious consequences. Because of the pivotal power of large urban states in presidential elections and the importance of urban centers within each state under the winner-take-all electoral-college system, contemporary Presidents have become attuned to the forces of urbanism, minority rights, and the social-welfare state. And because of his unique role as the "nation's sole organ in foreign affairs," the modern President must consider his foreign "constituencies." In contrast, the congressional power system places leadership in the hands of "those members . . . least aware of the problems of industrial society and least equipped to deal with them."[56] The reaction, localism, and delay of Congress acts as a brake on the progressive nationalism of the executive. Congress must be reconstituted if it is to participate in the policies of the President and his partisans "to save ourselves from nuclear destruction, help the world feed its children and protect their lands from totalitarian Communism, put our people to work and make our cities habitable, and realize the fact as well as the name of equality."[57]

Tenets of the theory. The executive-force theory seeks to mitigate Congress' "historic role of obstructionism."[58] First, Congress must recognize that "the executive is the active power in the state, the asking and the proposing power."[59] As a prominent liberal Democratic Congressman explains, "it is the natural thing for the executive branch to take the initiative, to make proposals, and to present us with programs."[60] Congress is "the consenting power, the petitioning, the approving and the criticizing, the accepting and the refusing power."[61] Second, Congress cannot administer or "man-

---

[55] Woodrow Wilson, *Constitutional Government in the United States* (New York: Columbia University Press, 1908), p. 68. See also Corwin, Chap. 1.

[56] Burns, *Congress on Trial*, p. 59.

[57] Joseph S. Clark, *Congress: The Sapless Branch* (New York: Harper & Row, 1964), p. 30.

[58] Clark, p. 235.

[59] Lippmann, p. 30.

[60] Chet Holifield (D-Calif.) in *Joint Committee Hearings*, Part 2 (1965), p. 185.

[61] Lippmann, p. 30. For a description of these congressional roles in military policy making, see Huntington, *The Common Defense*, pp. 123–146.

age and meddle'' in administrative provinces. As Joseph P. Harris
has cautioned:

> It is not the function of the legislature to participate in execu-
> tive decisions or share responsibility with executive officers, for
> which it is ill equipped, but rather to check on the administration
> in order to hold the officers in charge accountable for their deci-
> sions and for management and results.[62]

The executive-dominance theory thus emphasizes oversight as in
the 1946 Legislative Reorganization Act's injunction that congressional committees exercise ''continuous watchfulness'' over executive agencies within their jurisdiction. To prevent this watchfulness
from degenerating into meddling, however, executive theorists
usually specify that congressional review be in terms of generalized
policy considerations rather than details.[63]

Executive theorists point out, however, that congressional policy
initiation need not be wholly foreclosed. If the President fails to
act, or if there are gaps at the fringes of public policy, Congress can
and must serve as a ''seedbed for the breeding and maturing of new
legislative ideas.''[64] Senator J. William Fulbright's (D-Ark.) view
of the congressional partnership in foreign policy is a notable
example of this congressional role. He reasons that although
Congress is poorly equipped to participate in ''short-term policies
and . . . day to day operations,'' it can cooperate effectively in
debating ''longer-range, more basic questions'' and in initiating
ideas ''on the periphery.''[65] Fulbright's own record of initiating
policy alternatives demonstrates that this role need not be a
niggardly one.

Reform propositions. With the usual caveat on the complexity of
means-ends relationships in mind, an observer may expect proponents of the executive-force theory to advocate the following
reforms of Congress:

[62] Joseph P. Harris, *Congressional Control of Administration* (Washington:
Brookings Institution, 1964), p. 295. Also, see Walter Lippmann in *Newsweek*
(January 20, 1964), pp. 18–19.

[63] See, for example, Robert Dahl, *Congress and Foreign Policy* (New York:
Harcourt, Brace & Co., 1950), p. 143.

[64] Clark, p. 109. See also Holifield in *Joint Committee Hearings* (1965).

[65] For an exposition of the Fulbright viewpoint, see James A. Robinson,
Congress and Foreign Policy-Making (Homewood, Ill: Dorsey Press, 1962),
pp. 13 and 212–214.

A. Parties and the electoral system:
1. Reapportionment on the basis of population should be strongly supported on the assumption that elements of the presidential constituency (for example, urban and suburban areas) would thereby be strengthened in Congress.
2. National party councils to develop and implement a truly national party program should be strengthened; campaign finances should be centralized in the hands of the national committees.
3. Four-year terms that would coincide with the presidential terms should be enacted for Representatives. (Similar four-year terms for Senators would probably be desirable.)
B. The Presidency:
1. The 22nd Amendment should be repealed.
2. Funds for the executive branch should be appropriated on a long-term basis—two years or more.
3. The President should be granted an "item veto"—that is, part of a measure could be vetoed without nullifying the entire bill.
C. Congressional rules and procedures:
1. Congress should be required to act on all executive proposals within a specified period of time (for example, six months).
2. Strong, centralized congressional parties should be created.
3. The seniority system for selecting committee leaders should be discontinued, and elections by majority and minority caucuses should be substituted.
4. Individual Congressmen and Senators should be relieved of constituent "casework," and an Office of Administrative Counsel, under the general control of Congress, should be created to perform this service.
5. Congress should grant relatively broad mandates to executive agencies and should cease such harassing tactics as one-year authorizations or required committee clearances for certain executive actions.

PARTY-GOVERNMENT THEORY

Party government is the logical extension, and perhaps the end result, of the executive-force theory; but its roots and emphases are sufficiently distinct to warrant separate treatment. Actually, it is not a theory about Congress at all, but rather a proposal to reconstruct the American party system, so that a party would formulate a clear-cut and specific policy (platform) that would be responsibly effectuated when that party enjoyed a national major- ity. "The party system that is needed must be democratic, respon- sible, and effective," according to the academic manifesto of party government—the 1950 report of the American Political Science Association's Committee on Political Parties.[66] The basic malady of the American Congress is not myopic legislators or even archaic legislative rules and procedures, but rather the "parochialism of American life and the electoral system that fosters it." Thus, meaningful congressional reorganization can come about only through profound changes in the American party system.[67]

"An almost ideal form." The empirical foundation of party-gov- ernment theory is the familiar observation that American parties are unwieldy coalitions of parochial interests.[68] The party that is elected to power is incapable of organizing its members in the legislative and executive branches into a coherent, energetic, and effective government. The disorganization and parochialism of the parties debilitates the American political system. First, it renders impossible the "orderly, relevant, and effective politics" necessary in an era of urgent national and international problems.[69] Second, it perverts the concepts of the party platform and the public will. Frequently, a party, once in power, fails to effectuate even those programs which were delineated as electoral issues.

The Jeffersonian notion of popular majorities organized in national blocs or parties is the base of the party-government system. Such a system would have a tidiness unknown to the incoherent parties to which Americans are accustomed. A constant inspiration for many party-government theorists is the British party system, which Woodrow Wilson openly admired and which Burns calls "an almost ideal form of representative government."[70]

[66] American Political Science Association, Committee on Political Parties, *Toward a More Responsible Two-Party System* (New York: Rinehart & Co., 1950), p. 1.

[67] Burns, *Congress on Trial*, pp. 142–143.

[68] A discussion of theories of the political party is found in Samuel Eldersveld, *Political Parties: A Behavioral Analysis* (Chicago: Rand-McNally & Co., 1964).

[69] *Toward a More Responsible Two-Party System*, pp. 15ff.

[70] Burns, *Congress on Trial*, p. 110.

Coherent, democratic, and responsible parties would necessarily reflect themselves in strengthened party organizations on Capitol Hill. As the APSA Committee stated:

> A general structure of congressional party organization already exists. It should be tightened up. The party leadership in both houses already has certain functions with respect to the handling of relations with the President and the shaping of the committee structure . . . [and] other functions with respect to the legislative schedule. [These functions] should be strengthened.
>
> If such action were taken, it would not mean that every issue would become a party issue. It would not eliminate the need for or the possibility of nonpartisan and bipartisan policies. But it would result in a more responsible approach to party programs and a more orderly handling of *all* congressional activities.[71]

Such powers as committee appointment and legislative scheduling should therefore be centralized in the elective party leadership. According to Representative Bolling, "there is every reason to justify the right of the majority to have its major proposals voted on by the whole House without undue delay . . ."[72]

The authors of the APSA Committee's report were not optimistic about the prospects of "engineering consent" for such revisions. "It cannot be expected," they wrote, "that all congressional leaders will be sympathetic to the concept of party responsibility."[73] However, the committee hoped that nationally oriented Congressmen and Senators would take the lead in publicizing the cause of strong party organization. This hope is being partially realized in the writings of Senator Clark, Representative Bolling, and others of the "national" wings of both political parties who have worked to strengthen the party caucus and the elective leadership. Recent efforts to enhance the role of the congressional parties will be discussed in Chapter 5.

Reform propositions. Advocates of the party-government theory follow the executive-force theory in many respects but place particular emphasis on the following proposals:[74]

---

[71] *Toward a More Responsible Two-Party System*, p. 57 (italics in the original).

[72] Bolling, p. 242.

[73] *Toward a More Responsible Two-Party System*, pp. 88–89.

[74] *Toward a More Responsible Two-Party System*, pp. 57–64. See also Burns, *Deadlock*, pp. 327–332; and Bolling, pp. 239ff.

1. Control of congressional nominations and elections should be centralized—with national party clearance for candidates.
2. Congressional party leaders should be chosen after wide consultation among the entire "national" party, including the President.
3. Meaningful party policy committees should be created in each house; these committees should be responsible for legislative scheduling and for committee appointments conditioned on party loyalty.
4. Both Houses should schedule frequent party caucuses, whose decisions would bind members to vote the party line on important issues.
5. Committee assignments and chairmanships should be recommended by the party policy committee, ratified by the caucus, and subject to periodic review. Ratios of party membership on committees should favor the majority party.
6. Staff assistance should be provided both majority and minority committee members.
7. The House Rules Committee should be an arm of the elective leadership in scheduling measures for floor debate.
8. The present Senate filibuster rule should be altered to allow cloture of debate by a majority vote.

Conclusion: The Parliamentary Crisis

Divergent theories of the congressional function are the outgrowth of a complex, contentious society marked by numerous and often conflicting demands upon the institutions of government. Those citizens who urge upon the federal government an interventionist, problem-solving role will conceive of a legislature far differently than will those who see the government's role as a passive consensus-building one. The rules of the political game, as defined by the structure of institutions, cannot be divorced from the stakes for which the game is played. Moreover, these differing stakes are related to divergent intellectual interpretations of the role of institutions in a democratic polity. The theories of Congress should not be characterized merely as rationalizations for one's substantive positions; yet the two levels of debate are closely related. The struggle being waged over the character of Congress is indeed a part of the "war over America's future."

When the three theories are compared, a composite picture of

the American Congress emerges—a picture with important conver-
gences and deep differences. In this chapter's discussion, formal
"powers" of the legislature were consciously played down, in favor
of the broader and more fundamental concept of "function"—
those things of major consequence that an institution (in this case,
Congress) does for the political system as a whole. Table 1.2
presents a rough comparison of the functions specified for Congress
by the three theories discussed in this chapter, and the following
paragraph defines these functions as they have emerged from the
discussion.

TABLE 1.2

Three Theories of Congressional Functions

	Literary theory	Executive-force theory	Party-government theory
PRIMARY FUNCTIONS	Lawmaking Representation Consensus building Oversight	Legitimizing Oversight Representation	Policy clarification Representation
SECONDARY FUNCTIONS	Policy clarification Legitimizing	Consensus building Policy clarification Lawmaking	Lawmaking Legitimizing Consensus building

Lawmaking is the traditional task of deliberating, often at a
technical level, the actual content of policies. *Representation* is the
process of articulating the demands or interests of geographic,
economic, religious, ethnic, and professional constituencies. The
legislator may accomplish this through actual contact (residence in
a district, membership in a pressure group) or through "virtual"
means ("taking into account" a viewpoint, perhaps by anticipating constituent response). *Consensus building* is the traditional
bargaining function through which these various constituency
demands are combined (or aggregated) in such a way that no
significant constituency is severely or permanently disadvantaged.
Legitimizing is the ratification of a measure or policy in such a way
that it seems appropriate, acceptable, and authoritative. The
legislature promotes *policy clarification* by providing a public
platform where issues may be identified and publicized. *Legislative
oversight* is the review of the implementation of policy in order to
either alter the fundamental policy or introduce equity into the
application of laws. Other functions—for example, *constituent*

service and *recruitment of political leadership*—might also be explored, but are omitted here because they are not fundamental to the current debate over Congress.

The functions that theorists choose to emphasize have a profound impact upon the nature of the "model" Congress, not to mention the relationship of Congress with other elements in the political system. The most ambitious mandate is offered by the literary theory, which would involve the legislature at almost every step in the policy-making process—from initial conception to detailed review of implementation. In addition, this theory views the legislature as the prime representational and consensus-building institution in the political system. The executive-force theory, on the other hand, sees the legislature as ancillary to the executive establishment, which by the nature of things must assume the lead in both policy initiation and implementation. Like the board of directors of a corporation, Congress would have certain review powers but few operating powers; the legislature would find itself in most cases ratifying decisions of the executive "managers." According to the party-government conception, Congress (as well as the executive) would be set in motion by a strong and lucid party structure, serving chiefly as a forum for the staged confrontation of party ideologies.

No matter how far-reaching the consequences of accepting one theory over another, the differences in the concepts of the normative functions of Congress are differences of emphasis. Few observers would deny that Congress should, at one time or another, perform all the roles that have been discussed. Even the most dedicated advocate of executive dominance, for example, would undoubtedly concede that certain occasions may demand legislative initiative in policy making. Most theories of congressional functioning therefore admit to what might be called the "multi-functionality" of the institution. The priority assigned to these various functions then becomes the all-important question.

The implications of this chapter should by now be apparent. The present "parliamentary crisis" is primarily an absence of consensus on the priorities of the traditional functions of the legislature. The Constitution left the ultimate resolution of this conflict to the workings of history upon the precarious balance of powers. The changed environment of the twentieth century has intensified the question, even throwing into doubt the viability of legislative institutions. And the architects of legislative reconstruction cannot agree on the blueprints to be followed. The lack of consensus on congressional goals is suggested even by the nuances of wording: who could be mistaken concerning the philosophic distance between Burns' Congress of "anti-deadlock" and Burnham's Congress of "tradition"?

This lack of consensus constitutes a fundamental breach in the interlocking conditions for a rational-comprehensive approach to innovations in congressional structures and procedures. Lacking a substantial agreement on the expectations of congressional performance, observers will hardly concur on the specific shortcomings of Congress—much less the remedies to alleviate these shortcomings. The character and extent of the dissension on Congress among the public and among the legislators will be the theme of the next two chapters.

2 THE PUBLIC LOOKS AT CONGRESS

Belittling Congress is a venerable national pastime. Lord Bryce observed in the nineteenth century that "Americans are especially fond of running down their Congressmen." The other two branches of our government have nothing quite comparable to the public image of Senator Snort, the florid and incompetent windbag. Mark Twain, Will Rogers, Finley Peter Dunne, H. L. Mencken, Al Capp, and George Lichty have all contributed to the colorful literature of congressional denigration, presumably to the great amusement of their readers. Thus the current public criticism of Congress, however serious, is hardly a novel phenomenon: it is part of the American political folklore.

Congress is a public institution comprised of public men. It is a veritable goldfish bowl for the interested publics making demands upon it. Obviously, the aggregate attitudes of these publics are quite complex: physicians, glass-blowers, and tung-nut growers all presumably have their own thoughts about Congress in general and certain legislators in particular. These interested parties are ever confronting Congress with the eternal political question: "What have you done for me lately?" An individual's assessments of Congress and Congressmen are conditioned, from childhood, by a variety of factors—including his socialization into the world of politics, his perception of the saliency of politics, and his exposure to general and specialized media of political communications.

The Professional Kibitzers

Two groups that have a generalized, long-term interest in congressional performance are scholars of politics and journalists. By profession, both groups are uncommonly close to the legislative processes. By nature as well as by profession, both are conspicuously willing, if not eager, to broadcast their assessments of these processes. And both have regular access to rather wide and often important audiences.

Scholars. At least since the days of Woodrow Wilson, academic observers have shown an intense fascination with congressional organization and procedure. No accurate survey has been taken, but undoubtedly the professional political scientist is basically reform-minded. In early 1963, when Senator Clifford P. Case (R-N.J.) invited political scientists to respond to his proposed "Commission on Congressional Reorganization," he found overwhelming sentiment that "congressional reform is long overdue." Of the 195 political scientists who replied, 160 "strongly approved" of the Case proposal. Thirty-five were noncommittal, and none was opposed. Eighty-two percent of the scholars considered the proposed study "very timely and necessary."

"The failure of Congress" is a hoary theme that for years has been propounded by academics in textbooks and from lecture platforms. The congressional rogues' gallery—seniority, the House Rules Committee, filibusters, inefficient procedures, and so on—no doubt affirms the general impression among academics that "something ought to be done about Congress."

Scholars are less certain when discussing the appropriate roles Congress should play or the criteria by which Congress should be judged. Many in the political science fraternity have betrayed a distinct preference for the executive-force model of the congressional function. The historical reasons for this preference are revealing. First, since the New Deal at least, the executive branch has been a spokesman for the liberal values shared by many political scientists. Second, the executive embodies the expertise, specialization, and tidy organization so highly prized among academicians—many of whom have been schooled in the traditional techniques of administrative management. And finally, to the extent that political scientists have had governmental experience, they have been predominantly associated with executive agencies.

Academic spokesmen for strong party government, if not as numerous as the executive supremacists, have been at least as vocal. No doubt many of the values associated with the executive also have enhanced the attractiveness of party government; and the British party system has provided a constant inspiration.

The 1945 report of the American Political Science Association's Committee on Congress included several suggestions for a centralized party structure.[1] The following year, the Association appointed a 16-member Committee on Political Parties to launch a long-range investigation of party machinery and functions. In September 1950, this group published a report entitled *Toward A More Responsible Two-Party System.*[2] Strongly influenced by its chairman, Professor E. E. Schattschneider of Wesleyan University, the committee argued forcefully for "greater party responsibility" and thoroughgoing centralization of party machinery, including the party organization in Congress. The heated debate generated by the report soon died down because the report's brilliant intuitions on the ultimate evolution of American political parties were unmatched by its curiously naive philosophy of how these changes would take place. The academic profession's criticism of the report's empirical bases has negated its original impact, although vestiges of the party-government concept reappear in the writings of James M. Burns and others.

A sizable minority, especially among the younger and more behaviorally oriented political scientists, are mounting what might be called a tacit defense of many congressional practices. Through imaginative application of empirical techniques, these scholars demonstrate that certain practices and traditions that seem inefficient are actually useful in performing highly valuable but latent functions.[3] Thus the seniority system—generally viewed by academics as inefficient in utilizing the talents of younger members and undemocratic in reflecting members' views—is defended on the grounds that, by routinizing a potentially divisive set of decisions, it helps to reduce internal tensions in Congress. (Conflict reduction

[1] American Political Science Association, *The Organization of Congress* (1945).

[2] (New York: Rinehart & Co., 1950). See discussion in Chapter 1.

[3] Donald R. Matthews' perceptive analysis of "senatorial folkways" is perhaps the most notable item in this new literature on Congress: *U.S. Senators and their World* (Chapel Hill: University of North Carolina Press, 1960), esp. Chap. 5.

in a conflict-ridden institution like Congress is a very important function indeed and often results from practices not explicitly designed to do this service—hence, a latent rather than a manifest function.)

These political scientists are not necessarily captivated by the status quo and indeed represent a variety of philosophic and policy orientations. A few apply their research explicitly to the literary theory in one form or another;[4] others limit themselves to essentially empirical work that demonstrates, in general, that there is method underlying the seeming congressional madness. What unites these writers is a reaction against the traditional academic literature on congressional reform. One student sounds this theme with his observation that the "need [for congressional reform], though widely believed, is poorly sensed because so much exaggeration and misinformation about Congress passes for intelligence."[5]

Neil MacNeil, congressional correspondent for *Time* magazine, contends that this changed style of studying Congress has facilitated understanding between political scientists and political practitioners. Because of past criticisms, he says, Congress has often felt toward its academic critics the way the catfish must have felt toward the fisherman: "Hold still, catfish," the fisherman said, "I only want to gut you." For their part, political scientists are more sensitive to the congressional point of view than in the days of Woodrow Wilson. MacNeil notes approvingly the activities of those he terms the "Young Turks"—the political scientists who have frequented the committee rooms, lobbies, and corridors of Congress "and laid siege to the Congressmen to have them explain their actions and motives."[6]

In the wake of the much-maligned 1950 report and a decade of behavioralist analyses, a new examination of Congress launched by the American Political Science Association in 1964 confined itself largely to empirical investigation. Ralph K. Huitt, the director of the study, explained that "political scientists cannot offer really useful advice to Congress until we fill in some of the gaps in our

---

[4] To cite one recent example, a group of 13 scholars convened in 1965 to prepare working papers advocating reorganization of Congress along the lines of the literary theory. See *Congress: The First Branch of Government*, ed. Alfred de Grazia (Washington: American Enterprise Institute, 1966).

[5] Arthur Maass, "Congress Has Been Maligned," *Washington Post* (March 3, 1963), p. E 3.

[6] Neil MacNeil, "Congress and Its Critics," *New York Herald Tribune* (August 17 and 18, 1965).

knowledge of how Congress works.''[7] Although ''criticisms and
proposals are legitimate and necessary to the good health of
institutions,'' empirical research nonetheless has taught that
''there is great toughness in an established way of doing things.''[8]
Therefore, the study consisted of research topics subcontracted to a
dozen scholars who attempted to add to the body of basic knowledge
concerning Congress. As Huitt described the undertaking:

> Each individual scholar will be free to criticize and propose
> as he pleases . . . But what the study will not do is adopt a list
> of "official" recommendations which inevitably would be taken as
> the point of view of the discipline itself.[9]

The contrast between the 1964 study and the earlier reports of
1945 and 1950 reflects a fundamental change in the perspective of
the political science profession. But political scientists find themselves in an embarrassing paradox. Although they have more
confidence in their empirical tools now than a generation ago, they
remain divided in their assessments of Congress and have not as yet
produced the precise models of the institution from which prescriptive solutions can be advanced with assurance. Thus, academics
have been persuaded to concentrate on unfinished descriptive and
analytic tasks before taking on the kinds of broad prescriptive
ventures found in the earlier reports.

The press corps. Few people are closer to the daily activities of
the national legislature than the Capitol Hill correspondents. As
Charles Clapp remarks, ''Reporters probably have easier access to
the Congressman's time than any other group, largely because,
despite their shortcomings, they possess the power to advance—or
hinder—the Congressman's cause.''[10] Legislators admit that, in
addition to the public exposure so vital to them as elected officials,
they obtain valuable ideas from the journalists. On the other hand,
reporters typically have their ''sponsors'' on the Hill—Senators or
Congressmen who provide them with a flow of tips, leads, and

[7] Ralph K. Huitt, ''Congressional Reorganization: The Next Chapter''
(a paper presented at the annual meeting of the American Political Science
Association, Chicago, Ill., September 8–12, 1964), p. 1.

[8] Huitt, p. 4.

[9] Ralph K. Huitt, ''What Can We Do about Congress?'' *Milwaukee Journal*,
Part 5 (December 13, 1964), p. V 3.

[10] Charles Clapp, *The Congressman* (Washington: The Brookings Institution, 1963), p. 439.

information on the long-term issues as well as the day-to-day activities of Congress. Furthermore, the press exerts influence on the legislative process through its treatment of issues and events.

Growing out of the reporters' regular rounds on the Hill is the peculiar mixture of sarcasm and sympathy that they employ in assessing their news sources. ''Through close and regular contact and despite the cynical talk,'' writes Donald Matthews, ''reporters and [legislators] begin to identify with each other and to understand each other's problems.''[11]

In view of the relationship between the press and legislators, many reporters working on Capitol Hill could conceivably develop vested interests that would influence their attitudes toward their sources. Unfortunately, available data on the journalists' assessments of Congress are inadequate and contradictory. A mail questionnaire, distributed to the Washington press corps in the spring of 1963 by the seven Congressmen from Washington State, asked the newsmen to rate the performance of the President and Congress.[12] The 115 who responded answered as follows:

How Good a Job Is the President/Congress Doing?

	Excellent	Good	Fair	Poor	Don't know
President	16	52	33	13	1
Congress	1	17	38	50	6

Apparently the reporters were less than enamored with the congressional performance. As will be pointed out later in this chapter, the year 1963 was also marked by unusually low public support for Congress.

A survey of the press corps conducted a year later produced somewhat different findings. A random sample of journalists accredited to the congressional press, periodical, and radio and television galleries was asked to react to a list of statements concerning Congress. Of those responding to the question ''Which branch of the federal government is doing the best job?'' 35 percent selected the executive, 28 percent the judiciary, and only 14 percent the legislature. An additional 23 percent rated the three branches as ''about the same.'' But even though nearly two thirds

[11] Matthews, p. 213.

[12] The questionnaire was prepared by the Department of Political Science at the University of Washington and reported in the *Washington Post* (May 22, 1963), p. A 20.

of the correspondents thought that one or both of the other
branches was doing a *better* job than Congress, an even larger
proportion felt that, by and large, Congress was performing *well.*
Seventy-eight percent agreed or tended to agree that "In general,
Congress is doing a good job."[13]

Although the 1964 study indicated considerable agreement on the
quality of congressional performance, journalists, like scholars,
disagreed as to the proper role of the legislature. But in their
answers to a number of specific questions, the journalists were
interested in the prospects for congressional reform and concerned
about the inadequacies of the structure and procedure of the
legislative process. Like the political science fraternity, the press
corps appears to be a reserve of potential support for reform;
however, the mutual dependence of the legislator-reporter relationship probably dampens active reformism on the part of Capitol Hill
correspondents.

Dissemination of the news is an extremely complex process. Many
persons handle a story from the time the reporter telephones or
teletypes it from a congressional press gallery until the time that it
appears in print. Although these persons are usually free of the
restraints that Capitol Hill reporters encounter in dealing with
their sources, they face other problems—chiefly the limitations of
newspaper or magazine space and their publishers' political biases.
A full assessment of the image of Congress presented by the media
must await further research, which would include content analyses
of newspapers and periodicals. However, two tentative generalizations seem plausible: (1) in competition for space, Congress is at
a disadvantage with the more easily personalized Presidency,
because the congressional decision-making process is character-
istically fragmented and complicated; and (2) this same space
limitation may result in excessive simplification (in headlines as
well as in stories) of events on Capitol Hill and may create and
reinforce public stereotypes of Congress and the Congressman. The
shorthand device of identifying legislative items in terms of a
"presidential boxscore," for example, may contribute to an executive-force conception of legislative tasks. In many other ways, it is

---

[13] The survey from which these findings are taken was sponsored by the
Dartmouth Public Affairs Center under the authors' direction. A more detailed
analysis of press corps attitudes toward Congress will be presented in a later
volume.

probable that the media, consciously or not, influence the ways in which people think about their national legislature.

Editorial writers and commentators comprise one group whose views are not obscured. Because their personal contacts with Capitol Hill are less frequent than those of accredited reporters, editorialists might be expected to view Congress more critically. A cursory survey of editorial opinion would seem to confirm this supposition. A portion of the critical noise from the editorial pages may be attributed to the peculiar cycle of the normal legislative year. During the spring and early summer of each session, congressional work percolates in the committees and rarely breaks into the front pages. At this season of the year editorial pages blossom with such titles as "A Do-Nothing Congress" or "Torpid Spring on Capitol Hill" (to cite two actual examples). Then, as the summer wanes and bills are rushed to the floor, criticisms of congressional lethargy usually become less frequent.

Besides this seasonal phenomenon, editorial commentators voice a number of basic complaints about Congress. One critical school decries congressional "immobilism": the seeming inability of Congress to resolve political conflicts and produce legislation. These critics usually view Congress in terms of ideal efficiency and compare it unfavorably with the executive.[14] A second school of conservative editorial writers has attempted to counter the charges of inefficiency and illiberalism by stressing Congress' historic role in slowing down innovation and in developing a consensus. These writers denounce the pace of an activist Congress as "a frenzy of lawmaking."[15] Still another school consists of those reporters and columnists who specialize in exposing the foibles of Capitol Hill— Drew Pearson and his associates are perhaps the most conspicuous practitioners.[16] A criterion of "morality" marks their writings, and their special concerns include ethics, nepotism, junkets, and con-

---

[14] A handful of reporters especially close to Capitol Hill has been persuasive in expressing the "insider's" disdain for this type of criticism. See Tom Wicker, "It Is the People Who Face the Test," *New York Times Magazine* (December 8, 1963), pp. 19ff; also the columns of William S. White as well as his celebrated rhapsody on the Senate, *Citadel* (New York: Harper & Brothers, 1957).

[15] "It is no idle joke that a truly do-nothing Congress can sometimes be the best kind." Editorial, *Wall Street Journal* (August 4, 1965).

[16] Particularly controversial was Jack Anderson's "Congressmen Who Cheat," *Parade* (March 24, 1963), pp. 4–5.

flicts of interest. Their expectations for Congress—aside from rectitude—are unclear.

Radio and television are, potentially at least, as powerful as the printed media in influencing the public's view of Congress. The electronic media—networks and independent stations—obtain most of their material from the Capitol Hill correspondents and rely on wire-service staffs or in some cases their own reporters. Yet in all but a few cases, dissemination of the news is the responsibility of editors and announcers, who, far from the scene, face even greater problems than their counterparts in the printed media in compressing the stories into a few well-chosen words.

A simplified and stereotyped image of Congress is therefore often projected by the electronic media. Coverage is frequently haphazard and tends merely to reinforce general public images: by downgrading politics and the politician, as in numerous entertainment programs; by providing the Senate with more publicity than the House; and by providing the President with greater news coverage than either the Senate or the House. Occasionally, radio and television coverage of the legislature is very effective, as during the Senate filibuster against the 1964 Civil Rights Act. The evening news programs of CBS featured a daily report from Capitol Hill during which the news correspondent's image was superimposed over a clock showing the second-by-second lengthening of the Southern "holding action" against the bill. The networks can also highlight aspects of Congressional functioning which would otherwise escape public notice. In the fall of 1965, for example, NBC presented a special report, during prime viewing hours, on Congressional decision making.

In summary, the general view of Congress projected by the mass media is difficult to decipher. Certainly, any assessment of the role of the press must begin with the recognition that many different people are involved in gathering and disseminating the news. One hypothesis suggested by this discussion is that, for those reporters closest to congressional news sources, critical judgments of the institution are tempered by the very practical need to make sure that doors on Capitol Hill remain open to them. Those who must edit or interpret the news are not under such constraints, and may give wider play to their criticisms, or stereotypes, or both. Certainly writers and commentators have contributed to the public criticism of Congress, especially during the crucial 1963 period.

These generalizations are necessarily tentative, for research is sorely needed on the role of the press in mediating between political institutions and the public.

The Public's Image of Congress

The attitudes of "the public" are in a sense an aggregate of the attitudes of many specialized groups similar to those discussed above. Yet scholars and journalists are atypical in their interests and levels of information, and it is essential that generalized public-opinion data be considered. Unfortunately, surveys by scholars—so rich in the area of voting behavior—have little to offer on the public's attitudes toward the institutions of government. The late V. O. Key, Jr., struggled persistently with the problem of opinion "linkages" between citizens and governmental institutions, but the paucity of data made his effort primarily exploratory.[17] Commercial surveys must be relied on primarily, but they contain only sporadic references to Congress. During the years 1943–1965, for example, one well-known survey organization devoted approximately 10 questions to Congress but at least 100 questions to the Presidency. Nonetheless, a careful analysis of the available data reveals several significant findings that have not heretofore been exploited by students of Congress.

GENERAL AMBIVALENCE

Critics frequently contend that public disenchantment with Congress would be dispelled if only Congress would reform its structure and procedure. Perhaps caught up in his own enthusiasm for reform, one eminent observer has declared that "when Congress . . . reconstructs its machinery and methods to meet the requirements of modern times, then public criticism will subside and the prestige of our national legislature will be restored."[18] This observer's hope may be well-founded in the case of such vocal critics as scholars and journalists. But such a view begs the question of the actual level of public discontent, and implies a highly dubious explanation of the ways in which public opinion is formed.

[17] V. O. Key, Jr., *Public Opinion and American Democracy* (New York: Alfred A. Knopf, 1961).

[18] George Galloway, *Congress at the Crossroads* (New York: Thomas Y. Crowell, 1946), p. 293.

To put public attitudes in the broadest perspective, available evidence suggests that Americans take considerable pride in their governmental institutions. When asked what aspect of their country they admire most, Americans mention their governmental institutions more frequently than any other feature; Europeans, asked the same question about their country, more often speak of their nation's cultural heritage in art, literature, or music.[19] Moreover, citizens of this country express an uncommonly high sense of "civic competence." More than three quarters of the respondents in one recent survey believed that they had some recourse in overturning unjust laws—at the national level as well as the local level. Apparently, the American people see Congress as generally accessible to them.[20]

Yet this confidence in the American political system and its institutions does not necessarily carry over to the public's view of Congressmen themselves. In the first place, the collective style of decision making in Congress puts each Representative and Senator at a serious disadvantage in attracting public attention. People like to personalize leadership, and, to most people, Congress is a faceless body. Young children learn about the President before they acquire information about Congress; and this disparity of information about the two institutions continues through adulthood.[21] As one perceptive journalist has observed, the essence of news is confrontation. The operation of Congress, and indeed much of the infrastructure of American politics, is designed to diffuse and obscure this confrontation. As a result, the press and the public have great difficulty in comprehending congressional activity.

Certainly public knowledge of Congress is at best sketchy. In the 1958 elections, samples of voters in contested congressional districts were asked if they had "read or heard something about a candidate" for the House of Representatives. Considering the relatively low hurdle that respondents had to clear, the results are most instructive. Nearly one half of the respondents had virtually no knowledge of either the incumbent or his challenger (see Table 2.1). Added to the 15 to 20 percent decline in voting in nonpresi-

[19] Gabriel Almond and Sidney Verba, *The Civic Culture* (Princeton, N.J.: Princeton University Press, 1963), pp 236–253.

[20] Almond and Verba, pp. 185–186.

[21] Public information concerning Congress and the President is reported in Hazel Gaudet Erskine, "The Polls: Textbook Knowledge," *Public Opinion Quarterly*, 27 (Spring 1963), 137–140. On the perceptions of children, see Fred I. Greenstein, *Children and Politics* (New Haven: Yale University Press, 1965), pp. 61–63, 82.

TABLE 2.1

Voter Awareness of Congressional Candidates in 1958

		Read or Heard Something about Incumbent	
		YES	NO
Read or Heard Something about Nonincumbent	YES	24%	5%
	NO	25%	46%

Source: Warren E. Miller and Donald E. Stokes, "Constituency Influence in Congress," *American Political Science Review*, 57 (March 1963), 54.

dential election years, the evidence in Table 2.1 clearly indicates that the public has difficulty in identifying with its representatives.[22]

Perhaps the Congressman's image suffers less from his obscurity than from the fact that he is, after all, a politician—a profession which has a rather ambiguous status in the American culture. When former astronaut John Glenn decided in 1964 to parlay his public acclaim into a Senate seat, one Congressman lamented that many people were saying, "Isn't it too bad about that nice young man getting involved in that dirty business of politics." It may seem paradoxical that the public should hold such conflicting views of the institution and the people who make it work. But as William Mitchell explains, "Cynicism and idealism may be logically incompatible, but psychologically they are mutually supporting, indeed, necessary to one another. The American tends to expect the worst in politics but hopes for the best."[23]

[22] A 1965 Gallup survey reiterated that people have little information concerning even their own Representatives: of the nationwide sample of adults, 57 percent did not know the name of their own Congressman; 41 percent did not know his party affiliation; 70 percent did not know when he next stood for reelection; 81 percent did not know how he voted on any major legislation during the year; and 86 percent could not name anything he had accomplished for the district. (AIPO Survey [November 7, 1965].)

[23] William Mitchell, "The Ambivalent Social Status of the American Politician," *Western Political Quarterly*, 12 (September 1959), 695. These conflicting public evaluations pose a continuing dilemma for the Congressman. For the most part he shares the public's expectation that he will respond to popular sentiment. Yet in taking his cues from public opinion, he is faced with the impossible task of reconciling all manner of responses—from urgent pleas to disdain and hostility—which may even occur simultaneously. On the Congressman's ambiguous mandate, also see Edward Shils, "Congressional Investigations: The Legislator and his Environment," *University of Chicago Law Review*, 18 (Spring 1951), 572; and William Mitchell, "Occupational Role Strains: The American Elective Public Official," *Administrative Science Quarterly*, 3 (September 1958), 213.

THE EDUCATIONAL VARIABLE

Significantly, the better-educated Americans are among the most critical. A recent survey of college students (whose importance should not be minimized: by the 1968 elections one half of all citizens will be under 25 years of age) showed that they had only a

TABLE 2.2

Students' Confidence in Institutions

QUESTION: *"How much confidence do you have in these institutions?"*

Institution	Great deal	Only some	Hardly any	Not sure
Scientific community	76%	20%	2%	2%
Medical profession	73	22	5	–
Banks, financial	66	29	3	2
Supreme Court	65	28	6	1
Higher education	64	32	4	–
Big corporations	52	40	7	1
Executive branch	49	42	9	–
The arts	46	43	5	6
Psychiatric field	44	44	7	4
Congress	39	52	8	1
The military	38	43	17	2
United Nations	35	49	14	2
Organized religion	34	46	18	2
Civil rights movement	33	47	19	1
Democratic Party	22	63	10	5
The press	20	57	21	2
Advertising	16	38	44	2
Organized labor	13	55	29	3
Television	13	46	39	2
Republican Party	12	53	29	6

Source: Louis Harris & Associates, *Newsweek* (March 22, 1965), p. 45.

moderate level of confidence in Congress (see Table 2.2). The students rated the other two branches of the federal government somewhat higher than Congress and gave the two political parties a conspicuous vote of no confidence. In another survey, nearly two thirds of the college-educated respondents believed that members of the House were "mediocre types," and nearly half had the same low opinion of Senators (see Table 2.3). People at all educational levels thought more highly of Senators than of Representatives. Six

Gallup surveys in the years between 1945 and 1958 show that, in comparison with other educational groups, a consistently larger proportion of the college educated were dissatisfied with congressional performance. (See Table 2.4 for the data from the 1958 survey.)

TABLE 2.3

Education and Public Attitudes toward Legislators as Individuals

QUESTION: *"Would you say that most of the members now in the Senate/House of Representatives are high-type men, or that most of them are rather mediocre types?"*

SENATE

Respondents:	Grade school or less	High school or less	Some college	Totals
High type	41%	44%	43%	43%
Mediocre	27	36	47	36
Don't know	32	19	10	21
(Number of respondents)	(808)	(1093)	(602)	(2503)

HOUSE OF REPRESENTATIVES

	Grade school or less	High school or less	Some college	Totals
High type	36%	32%	24%	31%
Mediocre	31	45	65	45
Don't know	33	23	11	24
(Number of respondents)	(803)	(1093)	(603)	(2499)

Source: Roper Commercial Poll (May 1946). Courtesy of the Roper Public Opinion Research Center, Williamstown, Mass.

The manner in which the educated sector of the public views Congress is especially significant since these citizens tend to be the most active and most informed participants in political life. They have more information about their representatives;[24] and, on matters of judgment, their opinions tend to be more polarized than the less educated—that is, they show fewer responses of "don't know" when it comes to judging Congress and the Congressman. The

[24] The following proportions of adults in various educational categories knew the name of their Congressman in a 1965 nationwide survey: college, 62 percent; high school graduates, 43 percent; eighth grade or less, 32 percent. (AIPO Survey [November 7, 1965].)

critical members of the educated public represent a most demanding
constituency for Congressmen, but they also represent a most prom-
ising potential for support of Congress and of reform. However,
even assuming that they are attuned to the issue of congressional
reform, there would still be reason to doubt their willingness or
capacity to mobilize the much larger, more apathetic general public.

TABLE 2.4

Education and Assessments of Congress, 1958

QUESTION: *"In general, do you think the present Congress in
Washington has done a good job or a poor job to date?"*

EDUCATIONAL ATTAINMENT

	Grade school or less	High school (any)	Trade, tech., bus. school	College (any)	Totals
Good	26%	29%	53%	36%	30%
Fair	37	46	30	43	42
Poor	12	10	7	15	12
No opinion	25	15	11	6	16
(Number of respondents)	(502)	(729)	(57)	(269)	(1557)

Source: AIPO Poll (August 1958). Courtesy of the Roper Public Opinion Research Center, Williamstown, Mass.

CYCLICAL CHANGES

The American public's view of Congress is not static. Surveys
from 1943 to 1964 have revealed striking variations in the way
people view congressional performance (see Table 2.5). Prior to
1958, the level of public dissatisfaction with Congress (defined as
those saying Congress is doing a "poor job") ranged from a high
of 26 percent in April 1948 to a low of 5 percent in August 1955.
And surveys in December 1963 and December 1964 revealed a
sharp reversal of opinion in the course of a single year. The kinds
of discontent implied by these negative responses are not entirely
clear, but further analysis may suggest some of the correlates.
    Closer examination of the 20-year trends indicates three typical
response patterns, which are characterized in Figure 2.1. Public
approval is usually highest when domestic political controversy is
muted. In more normal times, approval is moderate and a sizable
minority is critical of Congress. When partisan controversy is
especially acrimonious, or when Congress seems slow in resolving

legislation, public disaffection increases. Although the 1963–1965 figures are not strictly comparable to the earlier data, such a crisis of public confidence apparently occurred during 1963 when much of the Kennedy administration's legislative program was stalemated on Capitol Hill.

During 1947 and 1948, when much controversial legislation was under consideration in Congress, the level of public disapproval

TABLE 2.5

Public Evaluations of Congressional Performance, 1943–1965

	Good	Fair	Poor	No opin.
March 1943	33%	29%	20%	18%
April 1944	27	45	13	14
October 1945	20	35	21	24
March 1947	21	36	25	18
April 1948	23	36	26	15
July 1953	33	35	14	18
August 1955	40	41	5	14
August 1958	30	42	12	16
October 1963*	34	—	49	17
December 1963*	27	—	51	22
December 1964*	58	—	33	9
December 1965*	62	—	26	12

* These surveys divided responses into only two categories—"positive" and "negative." They are by Louis Harris & Associates, *Washington Post* (January 6, 1964), p. A 1; (January 4, 1965), p. A 1; and (January 9, 1966), p. A 2. Other surveys are by the American Institute for Public Opinion and are used courtesy of the Roper Public Opinion Research Center, Williamstown, Mass.

was consistently high. As many of these conflicts subsided and the nation moved into the semimobilization of the Korean War, displeasure with Congress dropped considerably. The mid-1950s were a period of political quiescence; but by 1958, a year of recession and economic unrest, the public again began to be critical of congressional performance. Unfortunately, no relevant data are available for the 1958–1963 period; but one could speculate that public dissatisfaction dropped off again until perhaps 1962, then mounted gradually until the end of the first session of the 88th Congress (December 1963) when more than half of those interviewed were openly critical of Congress.

FIGURE 2.1

Attitudes toward Congress: Three Typical Patterns

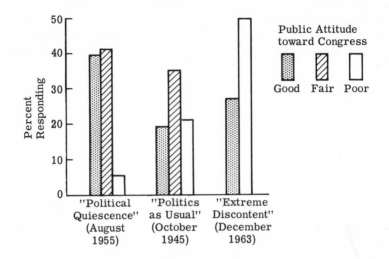

Source: AIPO and Louis Harris surveys (courtesy
Roper Public Opinion Research Center, Williamstown,
Mass.; and Louis Harris & Associates, New York City).

A different measure of public dissatisfaction is the rate of party turnover in congressional elections. Net party turnover in the House and Senate for each election year is strikingly parallel to the survey data on public dissatisfaction (see Figure 2.2). Over this 20-year period the civics class account of the democratic process seems, superficially at least, to describe the congressional electoral process: when citizens are disenchanted with the job Congress is doing, they express their feelings at the polls by removing incumbents and infusing the legislature with new blood; when public approval is high, partisan turnover diminishes. Thus in 1948, when more than one quarter of the respondents thought Congress was doing a "poor job," no less than 84 House and Senate seats changed parties—a net turnover rate of 15.8 percent. In 1956, not long after disapproval had dropped to 5 percent, the turnover was three seats—less than 1 percent. In 1958, after a summer of economic uncertainty during which public disapproval of Congress was climbing, the

FIGURE 2.2

Public Dissatisfaction and Congressional Party Turnover

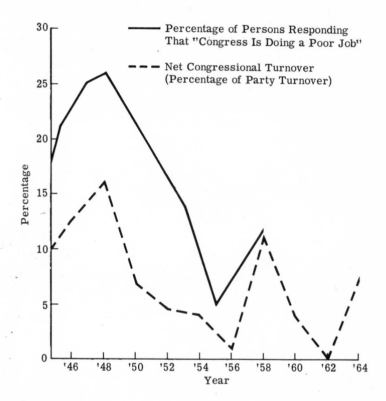

Sources: AIPO surveys (courtesy Roper Public Opinion Research Center, Williamstown, Mass.); *Congress and the Nation* (Washington: Congressional Quarterly, 1965), p. 63.

November off-year elections resulted in a turnover of 12.3 percent.

Of course, a rigid cause-and-effect relationship between public evaluations of Congress and election results is somewhat simplistic. Electoral decision making is complex and occurs within a broad political context.[25]

[25] See Angus Campbell *et al*, *The American Voter* (New York: John Wiley, 1960) ; and *Public Opinion and Congressional Elections*, eds. William McPhee and William Glaser (New York: Free Press of Glencoe, 1962).

LEGISLATION AND LOGJAMS

In general, the public expects Congress to pass rather than hold up legislation.[26] And to a much lesser degree, Congress is evaluated for the specific programs which it does or does not enact. Apparently, the continuous but often unglamorous operation of Congress in nonlegislative tasks (such as administrative oversight) goes largely unnoticed by the general public.

Respondents who were critical of Congress in December 1963 cited reasons that attest to the importance of blatant congressional *inaction* as a source of public disapproval (see Table 2.6). For

TABLE 2.6

Reasons for Public Satisfaction or
Dissatisfaction with Congress

NEGATIVE *(51% of sample)*

Not done much	21%
Avoided major bills	8
Too slow	7
Didn't cooperate with JFK	7
Everything stalled in committee	7
Civil rights bill not passed	6
Too much bickering	4
Medicare not passed	2
Not interested in people	2
Education bill not passed	1

POSITIVE *(27% of sample)*

Trying hard	17%
Passed some good bills	6
Making some progress	6
Blocked bad bills	4
An average Congress	2

Causes of Delays in
Congress (all of sample)

Southern Democrats	38%
Committee chairmen	21
Republican opposition	21
Democratic leadership	14
Northern Democrats	6

Source: Louis Harris & Associates, *Washington Post* (January 6, 1964), A 1.

[26] See, for example, AIPO Survey (January 6, 1959).

those expressing negative reactions to Congress (51 percent of the sample), the chief irritant was obviously the dilatory handling of the lawmaking function: "not done much," "avoided major bills," "too slow," and "everything stalled" were most frequently mentioned. Furthermore, three major unpassed proposals—civil rights, medical care for the aged, and aid to education—were cited by many respondents. And finally, congressional opposition to the President's program, a complaint that undoubtedly underlay many of the other negative responses, was mentioned by 7 percent of the group.

It is significant that no more than 4 percent of the sample endorsed the idea of legislative inactivity as a block to undesirable legislation—a major concept of the literary theory of congressional functions. In evaluating these figures, one columnist remarked that "the reason the country strongly disapproves the record of Congress is not because it dislikes the little it has done but because it believes that Congress has dallied, delayed, or failed to deal—for or against—the major issues." [27]

Specialized sub-publics, of course, tend to evaluate Congress in light of their own policy concerns. The proportion of respondents in three occupational groups—business executives, farmers, and skilled laborers—who stated that Congress was doing a "poor job" is shown in Figure 2.3 for the period 1945–1958. These lines follow roughly the levels of dissatisfaction in the total samples during the same period. However, the deviations of some occupational groups from the opinions of the total samples suggest that specific legislative programs influence group evaluations of congressional performance. For example, in 1947 business executives were more critical of Congress than were skilled workers; by the following year, these positions were reversed (see Figure 2.3). During this interval Congress passed the controversial Taft-Hartley Act, a measure strongly opposed by organized labor but generally supported by the business community. Similarly, during the period 1955–1958, when the Republican Administration and a Democratic Congress were having increasing differences over farm legislation, rural dissatisfaction with Congress jumped sharply. (Farm prices, relative to costs of living and farming, had declined considerably during those years.)

[27] Roscoe Drummond in *Washington Post* (January 8, 1964), p. A 11.

FIGURE 2.3

Percentage of Respondents Saying Congress
Is Doing "Poor Job"—by Occupation

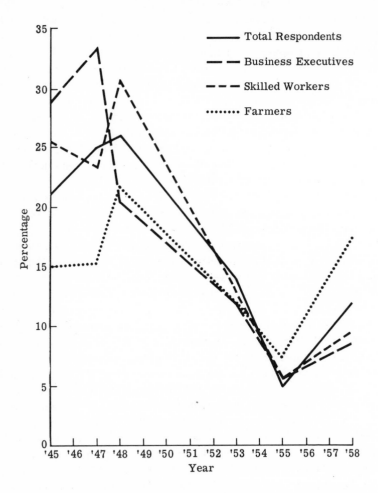

Source: AIPO surveys (courtesy Roper Public Opinion Research Center,
Williamstown, Mass.)

In short, public perceptions of Congress are related to the
personal benefits or hardships believed to accrue from specific
legislative actions. Apparently the public, to the extent that they
are aware of the issues, expect their representatives to follow

instructions rather than to exercise independent judgment.[28] Such views are also related to political party identification, a factor which is itself somewhat related to occupational classification.

THE SHADOW OF THE PRESIDENT

We have already noted that political scientists tend to favor the executive-force theory of Congress, that most journalists find the White House a more glamorous and rewarding news beat, and that much of the public expects Congress to act upon presidential initiative. Thus, to understand the public's attitudes toward Congress, a student must look also to the relationship between assessments of Congress and evaluations of the President. Assessments of Congress are heavily colored by the image of the President.

Figure 2.4 compares the relative frequency with which survey respondents have said that either the President or Congress is doing a "poor job." Survey evaluations of the President are even more variable than evaluations of Congress. (Minor variations in attitudes toward the President are not revealed in the graph. Although presidential surveys were taken every two months during the 1945–1958 period, only the ones made at the time of the five congressional surveys were selected for comparison.) However, a distinct parallel exists in the public's assessment of the two branches of the federal government. In 1948, when public discontent with Congress was at a high point, the proportion of people reporting dissatisfaction with the President reached a corresponding high point. And similarly in 1955, when only about 5 percent of the respondents rendered a "poor" verdict for Congress, only 13 percent expressed negative evaluations of the President's performance.

The available surveys unfortunately permit comparisons only between Presidents Truman and Eisenhower. Yet these two men had a strikingly different impact upon the public consciousness—a difference that is reflected in many of the charts in this chapter. Except for a temporary halo effect in 1945, induced by the wartime crisis and his dramatic accession to the Presidency, Truman's two terms were marked by acrimonious partisan strife and lively policy

---

[28] What evidence we have points to this conclusion. See Carl D. McMurray and Malcolm B. Parsons, "Public Attitudes toward the Representational Role of Legislators and Judges," *Midwest Journal of Political Science*, 9 (May 1965), 167–185.

FIGURE 2.4

Dissatisfaction with President and Congress

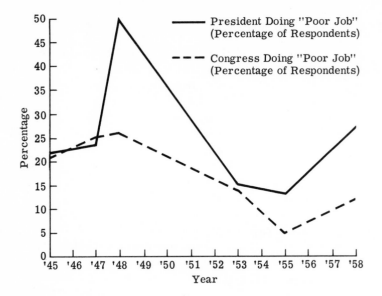

Source: AIPO surveys (courtesy Roper Public Opinion Research Center, Williamstown, Mass.)

debate in both domestic and foreign affairs. These conflicts took their toll in public restiveness toward both President and Congress. In comparison with his predecessor, Eisenhower was an unusually noncontroversial President. The clamor of interests did not cease, of course, but continued underground in the presence of a Chief Executive who as a national hero generated uncommonly favorable feelings from virtually all segments of the population. No doubt this feeling reflected itself in the relative contentment of the public with the two branches of government. (Yet, as Figure 2.4 shows, even the popular Eisenhower began to accumulate a sizable body of critics in the later stages of his Administration.)

Political-party affiliation should condition an individual's judgment of congressional performance. That is, a Congress controlled by one party ought to receive a more favorable evaluation from persons identified with that party than from those identified with the opposition.[29] Although the data collected throughout the 1943–1965 time period are not totally comparable, the surveys generally support this hypothesis—at least the relationship is valid in every case in which Congress and the Presidency were controlled by the same party.

TABLE 2.7

Party Identification and
Attitudes toward Congress

1948
(*Dem. President, Rep. Congress*)

| | | PARTY IDENTIFICATION | | |
		Rep.	Dem.	Indep.
ATTITUDE TOWARD	Good	24%	26%	18%
CONGRESS:	Fair	38	37	34
	Poor	24	21	33
	No opinion	15	16	15
	(Number of respondents)	(1181)	(1072)	(870)

1955
(*Rep. President, Dem. Congress*)

| | | PARTY IDENTIFICATION | | |
		Rep.	Dem.	Indep.
ATTITUDE TOWARD	Good	47%	35%	40%
CONGRESS:	Fair	39	44	27
	Poor	4	6	7
	No opinion	10	15	27
	(Number of respondents)	(600)	(800)	(14)

Source: AIPO surveys (courtesy Roper Public Opinion Research Center, Williamstown, Mass.)

In the three surveys taken during periods of "divided government"—that is, the White House and Congress were controlled by different parties—the results deviated somewhat from the expected pattern. Two of these surveys are reported in Table 2.7, which

[29] By referring to the discussion of ideological bases for evaluating Congress (Chapter 1), we might further hypothesize that "liberals" would fairly consistently rate Congress less favorably than "conservatives"; or even that Democrats would tend to be less favorable than Republicans in their evaluations. The available surveys unfortunately do not permit us to evaluate the ideological variable. As for the generalized level of responses by party, the best that can be said is that the data neither confirm nor disconfirm the hypothesis.

suggests that *supporters of the President's party tend to view Congress more favorably than do members of the "out" party, whether or not the presidential party also controls one or both houses of Congress.* When President Truman was dealing with a Republican Congress in 1948, a greater proportion of Republicans than Democrats expressed dissatisfaction with Congress. And in 1955, with a Republican President and a Democratic Congress, Democrats were more likely than Republicans to be critical of Congress. (The third such survey, taken in 1958, yielded results almost identical to those in 1955.)

If people were evaluating Congress on the basis of party identification, this phenomenon would not be anticipated. The most plausible explanation is that persons of the President's party blithely assume that their party is the government-in-power and that they evaluate all federal institutions accordingly. It is interesting that this phenomenon barely occurred in 1948. At that time the conflicts between President Truman and the "awful [Republican] 80th Congress" were relatively clearly defined. In contrast, Democratic Congresses of the early Eisenhower period took a position of "responsible opposition" in order to minimize the visible conflicts with the President. Thus in 1955, the public could not as readily differentiate the party in control of Congress from that holding the White House. The phenomenon indicated by the data in Table 2.7 is of the utmost significance, for it clearly suggests that Congress is not evaluated directly but rather through the prism of the Presidency.

This conclusion casts new light upon the apparent public acceptance of the notion of having the President and the majority in Congress represent opposing political parties. Respondents approving this "divided government" arrangement, according to one explanation, "tend to view it as a sort of built-in system of 'checks and balances' which . . . keeps both parties on their toes."[30] However, there is a distinct possibility that this sentiment was peculiar to the Eisenhower years. In fact, when Louis Harris reported the startlingly high disapproval of Congress at the end of 1963, he concluded that "there is little in the way of public response to the time-honored claim that the legislative branch is deliberative, carefully weighs the pros and cons, and, above all, is

[30] AIPO news release (August 25, 1959).

the guardian against excessive executive power.''[31] This apparent
lack of concern for the "separation of powers" may have been
influenced by the emotional aftermath of the Kennedy assassination. *Newsweek* magazine reported at the time that "much of the
sorrow still pervading the public over the assassination extends to a
feeling that Congress didn't do right by [President Kennedy].''[32]
But only a year later, President Johnson praised the legislators for
approving the bulk of the Kennedy program; and public confidence
in Congress rose considerably. In any event, the public has
displayed no stable, long-term commitment either to the party-
government concept or to the notion of balanced powers.

Summary and Conclusions

The leading questions posed in this chapter have been: What is
the extent of public dissatisfaction with Congress? And, how do
people arrive at their judgments concerning Congress? To answer
these questions we first detoured to consider the attitudes of two
relatively specialized groups—scholars and journalists. These
groups are undoubtedly more critical of the legislative process than
other segments of the population, and legislators are naturally
aware of this critical interest.

Congress apparently presents an ambiguous image to most of the
general public. As a primary institution in the governmental
system, it benefits from the general esteem which Americans hold
for their political institutions. Beyond this, the patterns of public
attitudes are complex and contradictory. For one thing, citizens
find it harder to identify with Congress than with the President. A
legislature's intricacies of structure and panoply of functions probably escape the perceptions of the average citizen. In many cases
this ignorance applies even to a citizen's own Congressman.

The public's ignorance of Congress results in assessments of
congressional performance that vary considerably over time and
are probably a function of party identification, interest-group
identification, or identification with the Presidency. And at least
for the time period 1945–1958, assessments of Congress were also

---

[31] *Newsweek* (January 13, 1964), p. 23.

[32] *Newsweek* (January 13, 1964), p. 23.

correlated with the ebb and flow of political issues. Satisfaction was highest during the mid-1950s when the President was highly popular, congressional relations were relatively benign, and political issues were somewhat muted. Satisfaction was also high during periods of national emergency with the concomitant diminution of political debate. On the other hand, public satisfaction was low in 1948 and again in 1963, when the Chief Executives had plunged into a welter of divisive policies, which were hotly contested on Capitol Hill.

Of particular significance is the finding that a large portion of the general public evaluates Congress by first assessing the President. Surprisingly enough, this identification is so encompassing that members of the President's party judge Congress more favorably even when it is controlled by the opposition. This finding held true even in the Truman Administration, when differences between the Democratic President and the Republican Congress were relatively clear and well-publicized.

What substantive expectations do people have of the role Congress should play in the political system? No doubt the rather general survey data currently available mask many nuances of opinion among the numerous sub-publics. Moreover, we are unable to assess the comparative weight of the several factors correlated with popular judgments.

Available data do suggest that the public expects Congress to cooperate with the President and to expedite major aspects of his legislative program. This propensity to judge Congress through perceptions of the Presidency only heightens the impression that the public's other expectations of the institution are vague and contradictory. On occasion, however, specific occupational groups hold views of congressional performance that deviate from the general opinion trends. These variations result from the differential impact, whether real or imagined, of policy decisions as filtered through the public press and through specialized, interest-oriented media of communications.

In the matter of specific reform proposals, the available surveys indicate that the public is relatively responsive to change. For example, no less than 65 percent of the respondents in a 1964 survey approved of the idea of requiring Senators and Representatives to disclose financial holdings.[33] On the issue of extending

[33] AIPO Survey (January 1964).

Representatives' terms from two to four years, the public has registered substantial approval—60 percent favored the proposal in late 1965, even before President Johnson included the issue in his 1966 State of the Union message.[34]

The notion of an "Ombudsman" to handle constituents' complaints has yielded more equivocal results. When respondents were confronted with the classic "Ombudsman" proposal—"an independent agency in Washington to handle the complaints of citizens who think they have not been treated properly by government officials"—42 percent thought it was a good idea, 29 percent a poor idea, and 29 percent had no opinion. An alternative proposal (similar to a suggestion by Representative Henry Reuss [D-Wis.]) for a congressional "Office of Administrative Counsel" received a 46 percent favorable response, with 41 percent opposed and 13 percent undecided.[35]

While hardly conclusive, these findings suggest that Americans are receptive to some congressional innovation. Though it cannot be inferred directly from the survey results, it remains probable that the general public lacks intense commitment on such specialized issues of reform.

What implications do these findings have for the politics of congressional reform? History suggests that public receptiveness to change is not equivalent to public pressure for change. Those rare occasions of public excitement over reform issues arise when issues are linked directly in the public mind with policy conflicts. The identification of Speaker Joseph Cannon with obstruction of progressive legislation during the first decade of this century, the House Rules Committee's blockage of a whole series of social-welfare measures in the late 1950s, and the inevitable association of

[34] AIPO Press Release (January 14, 1966). The question was: "How would you feel about changing the terms of members of the House of Representatives from two years to four years? Would you favor or oppose this?" A similar question in 1961 yielded 51 percent in favor, 34 percent opposed, and 15 percent with no opinion. See *Washington Post* (January 14, 1966), p. A 12.

[35] AIPO Press Release (December 3, 1965). The questions were: (1) "A proposal has been made to set up an independent agency in Washington to handle the complaints of citizens who think they have not been treated properly by government officials. Do you think this is a good idea or a poor idea?" (2) "As you may know, Congressmen spend about half their time doing errands and favors for people in their districts. To give Congressmen more time to consider new legislation it has been suggested that all letters and requests—except those dealing with policy matters—be turned over to a central bureau for handling. Does this sound like a good idea or a poor idea?"

the Senate filibuster with Southern opposition to civil rights legislation—these examples come readily to mind. For the public attitude during the insurgents' revolt against Speaker Cannon, we must rely on published historical materials;[36] in more recent times there is some evidence that the public identifies Congress' procedural problems with Southern obstructionism (see Table 2.6 above).

Congressional reform as an issue is undoubtedly most salient in times of political stalemate; yet it is precisely at such times that broad reforms are most difficult to effect because issues are intense, large legislative majorities are simply not available, and energies are consumed in more immediate policy conflicts. When the legislative process flows smoothly, impetus for reform subsides. However, we must not forget that whatever the judgments of professional critics and whatever the attitudes of the general public, questions of congressional reorganization must in the last analysis be confronted within the institution.

[36] See, for example, Kenneth Hechler, *Insurgency* (New York: Columbia University Press, 1941).

3 CONGRESSMEN VIEW CONGRESS AND REFORM

A democratic legislature worthy of the name should serve as a political crossroads of the community. And indeed, the notion of Congress as the "popular branch" suggests that, in contrast to other national governmental institutions, the working relationship between Congress and the American society should be especially direct and intimate. Here, petitioners of every kind may gather to state their cases and argue their causes, and the citizen has relatively free access to the offices, the corridors, and the committee rooms on Capitol Hill. On the other hand, the Supreme Court deliberates in magisterial isolation; and much of the work of the President and the executive agencies is cloaked in anonymity, if not secrecy.

In theory, the recruitment and election of legislators reinforce the close relationship between Congressmen and their constituents. For although there is a saying that Congressmen "never go back to Pocatello" once they have been caught up in the drama of Washington politics, it is also argued that many never really leave "Pocatello" or hundreds of similar home bases. In fact, there are stories, perhaps apocryphal, of members of considerable seniority (and representing constituencies distant from the capital) who have never spent a weekend in the Washington area.

Yet the people and their legislature are less intimate than traditional theory would have it. The findings in Chapter 2 suggest that the public views Congress, if at all, certainly through a glass darkly and with strong reliance upon more readily comprehensible referents, such as the Presidency. Likewise, the purpose and the problems of Congress look very different when viewed from the inside.

In general, the views of Congressmen are not in accord with the currents of criticism that are frequently generated by public discussions of congressional faults. But since legislators—whether from lack of time or from calculated disinclination—are less vocal than certain outsiders in evaluating publicly the strengths and weaknesses of Congress, available data on outside views of Congress (though far from complete) are far more conspicuous and comprehensive than information on views from the inside. This informational vacuum is a substantial barrier to an understanding of the present role and the possible future roles of Congress. The research effort reflected in this chapter was undertaken in order to gather, in systematic and quantifiable fashion, the Representatives' views on the topics of our earlier chapters: What is the appropriate job of Congress? How well is it currently performing? What are the principal defects in its operations?[1]

Views from the Inside

Congressmen are proud of their status and their institution. While many of them exhibit curiosity about outside evaluations, most assume a defensive attitude toward their institution. Scholars and journalists, our respondents told us, are naive and relatively uninformed about the day-to-day problems of life on Capitol Hill. Major news-gathering organizations, including Washington bureaus of major newspapers, the wire services, and the radio and television networks, were faulted by many Representatives for covering only a tiny fraction of the floor action, committee work, and behind-the-scenes struggles over legislation. Members of the House were frequently critical of editorial writers and columnists; Walter Lippmann, Roscoe Drummond, and Drew Pearson were often singled out—by different members and for different reasons. A substantial number of our congressional respondents felt that a combination of incomplete reporting and hypercritical commentary

[1] See Appendix A for a description of the field study, including a list of all questions in our interview schedule that generated the data employed in this and subsequent chapters.

helped to create a hostile public, thereby giving even more ammunition to Congress' outside critics.

CONGRESSIONAL THEORIES OF CONGRESS

Perhaps the simplest way to compare the views of Congressmen with those of outside observers is to determine the acceptability, within Congress, of our three models of the congressional function. As with outsiders, acceptance by Congressmen of the literary, executive-force, or party-government theories would normally be related to evaluations of current practices and of suggestions for change. To gauge the support for the tenets of the three alternative concepts, we asked members of the House four types of questions: (1) to describe the job of the Congressman as it ought to be performed; (2) to outline the functions which the Congress (and particularly the House) ought to play in the governmental system; (3) to list and discuss the problems they faced and the problems faced by the House as a whole in trying to meet the expectations that they had expressed in their first and second answers; and (4) to react to a list of statements concerning the work of Congress and Congressmen by indicating the extent to which they agreed or disagreed with each of the statements.

The Constitution serves as a powerful symbolic basis for action in the minds of many Congressmen and provides a strong argument for the literary theory as their frame of reference. In fact, when asked to describe the proper functions of Congress, more than one third of our respondents specified—with little or no elaboration—that Congress ought to "follow the Constitution" or "carry out our constitutional function—to legislate." Better than half (55 percent) of the respondents agreed with this brief statement of the literary position: "Congress and the executive should be equal partners in the making of public policy." But it was also clear that many thought one branch should be somewhat "more equal" than the others. Fully two thirds of the members interviewed assented to what has been termed the "Whig" variant of the literary theory: "Congress should play the major role in the making of public policy."

With so many members associating themselves in one way or another with the literary model of an active Congress, the popularity of the executive-force theory was predictably low. Nearly 70 percent of our sample disagreed with the proposition that "The executive should play the major role in the making of public policy."

The wide acceptance of the "Whiggish" variant of the literary model is further demonstrated when each member's responses to the

TABLE 3.1

Acceptance of Alternative Models of Congress
by Members of the House

Model or Variant*	Number of members	Percent of members
"Pure Whig"	27	31%
"Literary-Whig"	22	25
"Pure Literary"	8	9
"Literary-Executive Force"	9	10
"Pure Executive Force"	5	6
"Mixed"	15	17
No Data	1	1
	87	99%

* Member acceptance of the alternative models was determined on the basis of responses to statements numbered 10, 14, and 18 in question 3 (see Appendix A). "Pure Whigs" were those who agreed or tended to agree with 10 and disagreed, tended to disagree, or were undecided with regard to 14 and 18. "Literary-Whigs" were members who agreed or tended to agree with 10 and 14, but disagreed, tended to disagree, or were undecided on 18. Respondents classed as accepting the "Pure Literary" model were those who agreed or tended to agree with 14 and disagreed, tended to disagree, or were undecided on 10 and 18. Representatives who agreed or tended to agree with 14 and 18, but disagreed, tended to disagree, or were undecided in regard to 10 were listed as accepting the "Literary-Executive Force" variant. Finally, respondents agreeing or tending to agree with 18 and disagreeing or tending to disagree with 10 and 14 were considered as accepting the "Pure Executive Force " model. All other response patterns were considered "Mixed."

three alternative models are combined and his overall attitude is characterized, as in Table 3.1. A majority of the Representatives espoused the "congressional supremacist" variant of the literary theory. On the other hand, a substantial group (17 percent) in the House indicated no clear preference among the competing models.

Further clarification of congressional views of the alternative theories of Congress resulted from our respondents' discussions of their major problems. It became clear that House members considered even the limited operation of the executive-force model as a major barrier to the proper performance of their perceived roles. About one half of the Representatives interviewed mentioned some form of executive branch "encroachment" as a complicating factor in their legislative work. Further, problems stemming from the contemporary operation of the separation of powers—principally conflict with the executive branch—were the second most frequently mentioned type of problem interfering with the proper functioning of the individual member and of the House as an institution.

Since executive-force theory advocates are often among the most publicly visible members of the House, outsiders underestimate the extent to which the theory is rejected within Congress. The advocates of executive initiative are inveterate speechmakers and prolific writers. Because of their frequent public expressions, their point of view appears more widely held among members than it actually is. And some Congressmen claim that executive-oriented members are better able to have their views reported and circulated in the public media, since editors themselves tend to share their position.

Our survey data clearly confirm, however, that Representatives embrace the idea of an active role for Congress and desire to strive for at least an equal status with the executive. Even a John McCormack or a Carl Albert in the House and a Mike Mansfield or a Mike Monroney in the Senate—all staunch fighters for a Democratic administration on most issues—will oppose the President and his advisors upon occasion in order to uphold their personal or institutional prerogatives. The same was true of Republican legislators during Eisenhower's tenure in the White House. The great majority of Congresmen, however "liberal" and/or nationally oriented, apparently take seriously the notion that the Constitution is not really a document of separate powers, that, rather, it is an invitation—given with much forethought—for Congress and the President to struggle for the sharing of power. Few legislators recoil from this struggle.

An earlier discussion indicated that often only a fine line distinguishes the executive-force from the party-government theory. Political analysts talk in the same breath about strong parties and strong presidential leadership of parties. Many of the trends in American politics which point toward executive supremacy in government policy making also imply a stronger role for the President as chief of his party.

Many Congressmen, however, see a real and significant difference between strong parties *per se* and executive-branch domination of those parties (and therefore of Congress). The preference for a stronger Congress *and* stronger parties, for example, could be seen in the replies of many of the Congressmen—although the great majority of members could scarcely be classified as ardent advocates of thoroughgoing party government. Widespread pro-party sentiment was evidenced in reactions to the more modest party-oriented propositions. For example, two thirds of our sample disagreed with the statement, ''Under our form of government every individual should take an interest in government directly, not through a political party.'' And there was an even stronger reaction against the idea of reducing the role of parties in elections. The proposition that ''The best interests of the people would be better served if Congressmen were elected without party labels'' was rejected (often with obvious horror) by 86 percent of the respondents.

When more demanding criteria for the party-government model were employed, the number of advocates dropped off considerably. On the question of whether ''the two parties should take clear-cut, opposing stands on more of the important and controversial issues,'' the members interviewed were split almost evenly (51 percent opposed the statement) ; and on the question of voting with one's party leadership at the cost of some district support, the party advocates fell to 38 percent.

But it does seem apparent that many members of the House would be sympathetic to a somewhat strengthened congressional party system. A substantial minority (45 percent) of our respondents gave a pro-party government response to at least three of the four propositions mentioned.[2]

The relative consensus that emerges from these congressional opinions differs substantially from most of the outside views of Congress listed in the previous chapter. Congressional preference for the literary theory over the executive-force theory is easily explained in terms of institutional loyalty. Not so easily explained is the substantial minority of Representatives who combine the rejection of executive dominance with the advocacy of at least a modicum of strong party organization.

---

[2] We would place the strength of the ''hard-core'' party-government advocates in the House during the 88th Congress at about 15 percent of the membership. This 15 percent is the proportion of our random sample that gave an unambiguous pro-party-government response on all four of the propositions.

This desire for a stronger congressional party system cannot be explained as merely a device to elevate the legislature and to frustrate the executive. After all, congressional obstacles to the President's legislative program are frequently erected by small groups of strategically situated Congressmen operating independently of party leadership. We suggest that a commitment to active legislative parties does not necessarily imply the negativism that is often ascribed to congressional opponents of the executive-force theory. On the contrary, it may simply reflect the feeling that strong congressional parties with collective responsibility are essential for maintaining a political dialogue among the branches of the national government. Congressional party advocates hold that this dialogue is lacking when the President calls all the shots in public policy—just as when a "do-nothing" Congress opposes a President's programs without suggesting alternatives of its own.

CONGRESSMEN DEFINE THEIR ROLES

The congressional interpretation of the three theories of Congress is not the only discrepancy between inside and outside views of our national legislature. Naturally, Congressmen are able to provide more detailed observations on legislative life than are available in most public discussions. The members of Congress have opinions not only about the role of Congress but also about the finer details of an individual member's approach to his job.

Much of our information on the Congressmen's perceptions of the role of the individual member comes from a series of questions in which each Representative was asked to define, in his own words, "the job of being a Congressman—what are the most important things you should do here?" The responses permitted analysis along a number of dimensions: the kinds of activities in which he spent great blocs of time while in Washington; the principal roles which he felt he ought to play in the legislative process; how he defined the constituency which he represented; and the manner in which he went about representing this constituency.[3]

One critical segment of the legislator's role has been termed the "purposive" or goal-oriented dimension: the member's interpretation of the ultimate aims of his activities, of "the where-from or

[3] The role typologies employed in this study were adapted from intensive research on state legislatures. See John C. Wahlke, Heinz Eulau, William Buchanan, and LeRoy C. Ferguson, *The Legislative System* (New York: John Wiley, 1962), esp. Chapters 1 and 11.

what-for of legislative action.''⁴ The variety of ways in which this
role was defined by our respondents illustrates the diversity of
perspectives which must be considered in an evaluation of Congress
and its future.

The most frequently articulated purposive role was that of the
''Tribune''—defined as determining, representing, or protecting
the interests of ''the people.'' (See Table 3.2 for data on the
frequency with which specific role interpretations were invoked in
our interviews.) The second most common role was that of the
''Ritualist,'' who defines the legislator's prime duties in terms of
the formal ''textbook'' activities, such as floor debate, voting on
proposed legislation, hearings, investigations, and other committee
work. Next in frequency was the role of the ''Inventor''—the
problem solver who views his task as the formulation of specific
policies for the general welfare. (Although Inventors were typically liberals, conservative Inventors were also represented in our
sample. Consider the case of the Midwestern Republican who had
his own unique solution for all the fiscal problems of the national
government. Place executive agencies and the Treasury on the
double-entry bookkeeping system, he said, and all tax, spending,
debt, and executive-oversight problems would be brought under
control.) The fourth purposive role was that of the ''Broker''—the
legislator who sees his job as a weighing and balancing of the many
competing interests that strive for policy advantages. The ''Opportunist'' role was the least frequently articulated and also the most
limited in its focus: campaigning and gaining reelection (or
further promotion of a political career). The problem of being
reelected is never far from the consciousness of most Congressmen.
The difference between Opportunists and the others was well stated
by a former Representative: ''All members of Congress have a
primary interest in being reelected. Some members have no other
interest.''⁵

It is evident that the insiders' views of the proper role of a
Congressman and of his institution are as diverse as the views of
those who appraise congressional functioning from the outside.
Though not totally contradictory (many members, in fact, expressed more than one purposive role), the diverse opinions among

⁴ *The Legislative System*, pp. 12 and 243.
⁵ Frank E. Smith, *Congressman from Mississippi* (New York: Pantheon
Books, 1964), p. 127.

Congressmen on the "proper" role of a member lead to divergent views on proposed changes in congressional structure. In this manner the persistent party and policy differences among legislators are reinforced by differences in their orientations toward congressional policy making. The typically slow pace of legislative procedures may frustrate the Inventor who is filled with the need to

TABLE 3.2

Distribution of Purposive Roles among
87 Members of the House

Role	Percent of members*	Percent of all roles mentioned
Tribune	82%	40%
Ritualist	67	33
Inventor	31	15
Broker	17	8
Opportunist	8	4
		100%

* Since many members articulated more than one role, the sum of the percent of members indicating all of the roles considerably exceeds 100 percent.

get things done, but these same procedures may be quite satisfying to the tradition-oriented Ritualist as well as to the Broker, who is striving for more time to make honest bargains among conflicting interests.

WHAT CONGRESSMEN COMPLAIN ABOUT

We have noted that many members assume a defensive attitude toward Congress when it is under attack. Congressmen naturally display great pride in and affection for the legislative branch and are far less likely than outsiders to criticize it. On the other hand, the members collectively share their fellow citizens' uncertainty as to what Congress should do or be—as attested by the lack of agreement on the appropriate model of Congress and the proper purposive role for its members.

Given the diversity of the normative roles that they assign to themselves and to Congress as a whole, many members are understandably dubious about the extent to which they, and Congress as a whole, are able to meet their expectations. Table 3.3 indicates that the vast majority of members in the 88th Congress were neither completely satisfied nor completely dissatisfied with their own ability, or that of the institution, to perform as they thought they should. If we were to speak of a "typical" evaluation, we would say that it consists of a moderate to high level of satisfaction coupled with specific complaints about *both* individual and institutional

TABLE 3.3

Member Satisfaction with Personal and Institutional Performance

| | | *Satisfaction with Institutional Performance*** | | | |
		LOW	MODERATE	HIGH	TOTALS
*Satisfaction with Personal Performance**	LOW	7%	4%	1%	12%
	MODERATE	7	48	17	72
	HIGH	2	7	7	16
	TOTALS	16%	59%	25%	100%
(Number of respondents)		(14)	(50)	(22)	(86)***

* Derived from responses to questions 1(a) and 1(b), Appendix A.
** Derived from responses to question 2(b), Appendix A.
*** One of the 87 respondents could not be classified on either of the dimensions of satisfaction with performance.

performance. The vote in the House on the quality of Congress would seem to be "aye—with reservations."

What are these reservations? What are the problems about which members of the House feel free to complain? We asked each of our respondents to list and discuss "the most pressing problems you face in trying to do your job as Congressman" and "the most pressing problems which prevent Congress from doing what you think it ought to do." The result was a formidable list of complaints and problems—more than 600 in all. (On the average, each member interviewed mentioned seven or eight problems.) An examination of Table 3.4 shows, not surprisingly, that Congressmen are as divided about what is wrong with Congress as they are in describing what their jobs—and Congress—should be like.

The inventory of members' complaints provides only partial assistance in understanding the likely structure and functions of a Congress of the future. Many of the problems cited by Congressmen relate to conditions which are only marginally, if at all, susceptible to reform. The most frequently mentioned problems were associated

TABLE 3.4

General Categories of "Problems" Articulated by
Members of the House of Representatives*

Type of problem	Number of times mentioned	% of all problems	Number of members mentioning	% of all members
1. Committee system, seniority system, and Rules Committee	38	6%	26	30%
2. Scheduling and general procedure	54	8	36	41
3. Member pay, office allowances, staffing	29	4	21	24
4. Diffusion of leadership and "failure" of incumbent leadership	19	3	17	20
5. Caliber of individual members	38	6	27	31
6. Problems stemming from present operation of separation of powers	84	13	48	55
7. Problems of House-Senate comity	9	1	9	10
8. Public lack of understanding of Congress and failure in communication with constituents	54	8	36	41
9. Service for constituents	59	9	50	57
10. Electoral system and electoral vulnerability of members; campaigning	86	13	44	51
11. Complexity of decision making; lack of information	78	12	54	62
12. Criticisms of present power distribution and policy output of the House	63	10	42	48
13. Lack of time**	34	5	32	37
14. Other	14	2	14	16

* Based upon a random sample of 87 members of the 88th Congress. The fourteen categories in Table 3.4 are general and mask many important qualitative differences. Each member interviewed was asked to name any problems that prevented him from carrying out the role he would like to play in the House and all problems that prevented the House from operating as he thought it should. We have analyzed a maximum of ten problems mentioned by any one member (a few mentioned more): five personal and five institutional problems.

** Because "lack of time" is such an obvious and commonplace problem, we excluded it from analysis whenever a member mentioned his "quota" of ten other problems. The category is therefore underrepresented in this table.

with the complexity of decision making: the lack of information, the volume of legislation to be considered, and the difficulty of making a rational choice from among many conflicting alternatives. These problems are a concomitant of policy making in the modern world under any set of rules and within any complex and responsible organization. We can classify more than one fourth of the problems (Table 3.4, items 11, 12, and 13) as endemic—that is, inherent in a system where men and women of finite capacity grapple with issues and difficulties of nearly infinite dimensions. Also high on the list of complaints were the classic dilemmas of the Representative: getting reelected and maintaining good relationships with constituents.

Another group of problems, constituting more than 50 percent of those mentioned, relates to the capabilities of House leaders, the quality of individual members, and the characteristics of the overall electoral system (Table 3.4, items 4–10). Many of these problems— barriers to the ''proper'' functioning of the individual member and of the total institution—could in theory be removed, but most of them are of a scope which is far broader and more fundamental than that usually embraced by proposals for congressional reform. The remaining 20 percent could be categorized as problems of internal congressional reorganization (Table 3.4, items 1, 2, and 3). These topics—the operation of the committee system, scheduling, staffing, and the prerogatives of seniority—compose most of what is normally thought of as congressional reform. This group of problems, although relatively small, is far from insignificant; few people would be unhappy in a world where one fifth of all their problems were removed.

Attitudes toward Reform

Congressmen sometimes appear to be as concerned with changing their institutions as the most active and articulate outside reformers. Congressmen of differing political colorings—from an Eastern liberal Democrat like Senator Joseph Clark to a Midwestern conservative Republican such as Representative H. R. Gross—voice persistent and vociferous complaints about the conduct of legislative business. These men claim not only that Congress frequently makes unwise decisions but that it makes them unfairly and inefficiently. In every session of Congress, several score of bills and resolutions are introduced to modify the rules and structure of one or both houses. In 1965, dozens of Senators and Representatives took time from an especially active legislative session to testify before the Joint Committee on the Organization of the Congress.

Despite this apparent evidence of members' interest in reform, the fact remains that in the years between 1946 and 1965 there were few major changes in the central body of rules and procedures by which legislative business is carried on. Apparently, the reformist ''noise'' that emanates from Capitol Hill is largely sound (if little fury) signifying little about the real disposition of Congressmen to work for reform. Senator Everett M. Dirksen may have voiced the private thoughts of many of his congressional colleagues when he responded to one proposal for change with ''Ha, ha, ha, and I might add: ho, ho, ho.''[6]

MEASURING REFORMISM

Assessing the true temper of the Congress toward reform is no mean task. Public professions of interest in the subject are certainly misleading if (as is often the case) the talk is not backed up with action. On the other hand, the seeming fixedness of accepted procedure does not preclude the possibility that there may be a substantial number of Congressmen who favor certain reforms but who have been unable, for one reason or another, to achieve their goals.

One way of discovering Congressmen's actual preferences is to ask them. In our interviews on Capitol Hill, members of the House of Representatives provided us with their reactions to a list of proposed legislative reforms. The 32 items on the list were a representative sample of the hundreds of proposals for change advanced by political scientists, journalists, members of Congress, and others.[7] This sample included suggestions for insuring congressional equality (at the least) in policy making, as advocated in the literary model; for buttressing the power of the President along the lines of the executive-force model; and for strengthening and clarifying the role of the parties, as suggested by the party-government model. The list also included a number of reform

---

[6] See Meg Greenfield, ''Everett Dirksen's Newest Role,'' *The Reporter* (January 6, 1964), p. 29.

[7] The list of 32 reform proposals can be found in Appendix B.

proposals which, if effected, would probably not alter substantially the weight of Congress in the political system. These suggestions would change somewhat the power structure within Congress and would make the legislator's life more orderly and perhaps less frustrating.

A Representative's combined responses to all 32 proposals give us a crude indication of his general predisposition to reform. The

TABLE 3.5

Level of Support for 32 Reform Proposals among
Members of the House of Representatives

Percentage of reform items supported*	Number of members	Percentage of members
0–19%	7	8%
20–39%	25	29
40–59%	32	37
60–79%	19	22
80–100%	3	4
Totals	86**	100%

* Excluded from the computations were all items on which respondents were undecided or failed to reply in any way. Thus the "percentage of items supported" by each respondent was derived by dividing the number of items he supported by the sum of the number of items he supported and the number he opposed.

** We were unable to obtain the attitudes of one of 87 respondents toward any of the 32 proposals on the list.

combined responses of all those interviewed in turn provide evidence as to the extent of "reformism" within one of the two houses of Congress.

The most obvious finding is that a strong commitment to institutional reform is not the dominant mood of the House. When our respondents were placed into five groups ranging from the least to the most frequent support of reform items (see Table 3.5), few were located at the pro-reform end of the scale. Only slightly more than one fourth of the respondents gave their assent to a substantial majority (60 percent or more) of the reform items. To be sure, a sizable number of Congressmen were to be found in the middle ranges, supporting about as many of the proposals as they opposed.

But a bloc of equal size was clearly opposed to the bulk of the suggested reforms.

Anticipating later discussion somewhat, we might also note that there is only scattered support for the most significant of the specific changes. Of the 14 items which received the support of a majority of responding members, only three could be considered substantial modifications of the power structure and the decision-making processes within the House (items 5, 7, and 14 in Appendix B).

WHO ARE THE REFORMERS?

Before considering in detail the constellation of forces surrounding specific reforms, we will try to identify some of the apparent determinants of both pro- and anti-reformism by sketching collective portraits of two groups of Representatives—those most strongly favoring reform and those most strongly opposing it.[8]

The stimuli to oppose or support the general notion of reform apparently stem from sources other than a Congressman's personal and social background. Congressmen are drawn from many walks of life and from all sections of the nation; they bring to the legislature a wide variety of educational attainments. Further, the job of Congressman is, if not the top of the career ladder, certainly the result of a climb through many lower-rung political jobs in the home community and state. From the extensive theorizing about the behavior of political decision makers,[9] one might well expect that persons with differing educational, occupational, and political backgrounds would vary in their reactions to congressional reform. But with few exceptions we found that it makes little difference in a Representative's predisposition to support reform whether he is a high school or a college graduate; whether he is a lawyer, a businessman, or a member of some other professional or vocational grouping; or whether he has served an extensive or limited political apprenticeship before entering the House.

However, when we considered the more explicitly political

[8] The group strongly supporting reform includes all respondents favoring at least 60 percent of the items. Members in the group classed as opposed to reform include all those favoring fewer than 40 percent of the proposals. (See Table 3.5.)

[9] See, for example, Donald R. Matthews, *The Social Background of Political Decision-makers* (Garden City: Doubleday, 1954).

environments of our respondents, we encountered some noticeable differences. Democrats were overrepresented among the group favoring at least 60 percent of the 32 reform items. Republicans, on the other hand, were more likely to fall in the moderate reform group (that is, supporting 40–59 percent of the proposals). Congressmen from the Southern states were more strongly opposed to the general notion of reform than were members from any other region. More than two thirds (69 percent) of the Southerners in our sample fell into the group supporting less than 40 percent of the reorganization proposals, and only four percent of the Representatives from that region favored at least 60 percent of the items. Westerners, on the other hand, were considerably overrepresented in the group strongly favoring reform and underrepresented among those opposed to most of the proposals.[10] Members representing urban districts were far more supportive of reform than were those from rural areas. In fact, over half of those members approving 60 percent or more of the proposals came from city districts, while over half of those supporting less than 40 percent of the items came from rural constituencies.[11] There was also a tendency for Congressmen from the more competitive districts to look with greater favor on the list of reforms than did members from less competitive or one-party constituencies.[12]

These data suggest that the placement of Representatives on an ideological scale of liberalism and conservatism might help to explain their attitudes toward reform. This is indeed the case. Defining conservatism in terms of the level of support for the so-called ''conservative coalition,''[13] we found that the most conserva-

[10] The definition of regions is from the *Congressional Quarterly*. See *Congressional Quarterly Almanac, 1962* (Washington: Congressional Quarterly Service, 1962), p. 740.

[11] The classification of district type is from the *Congressional Quarterly Almanac, 1963* (Washington: Congressional Quarterly Service, 1963), pp. 1170–1184.

[12] Competitive districts are those in which the winner received less than 60 percent of the vote in the November 1962 congressional election. The voting data employed in the calculations are from the *Congressional Quarterly Almanac, 1963* (Washington: Congressional Quarterly Service, 1963), pp. 1123–1161.

[13] For a definition of the ''conservative coalition'' as well as data concerning support of that coalition, see *Congressional Quarterly Almanac, 1964* (Washington: Congressional Quarterly Service, 1965), pp. 745–753. We have computed a coalition-support score for each of our respondents by dividing the percentage of times each supported the coalition in the 88th Congress by the sum of his coalition-support percentage and his coalition-opposition percentage. This procedure removes the effect of absences during roll-call votes.

tive members tended to be least supportive of reform, while a
majority of liberal Representatives favored 60 percent or more of
the reform proposals (see Table 3.6).

These data permit the tentative conclusion that Congressmen who
constitute the backbone of the reform movement in the House of
Representatives come from districts more desirous of positive
legislative action and have the most active and demanding constitu-

TABLE 3.6

Support for "Conservative Coalition" and
Support for Reform of the House

*Support for "Conservative Coalition"**

Percentage of reform items supported	LOW (0–19%)	MODERATE (20–79%)	HIGH (80–100%)
0–39% (Low)	8%	42%	57%
40–59% (Moderate)	40	39	33
60–100% (High)	52	19	10
	100%	100%	100%
(Number of respondents)	(25)	(31)	(30)

* See footnote 13 for a definition of "conservative coalition" support.

ents, the most precarious political positions, and the most consistently liberal policy orientation. They "feel the heat" from their
constituents and thus have strong personal motives for desiring
change. The difficulties encountered by these members in trying to
satisfy personal and constituency demands may lead them to opt
for changes in the structure and procedures of Congress, changes
which they feel will enhance the chances for passage of legislation
which will assuage their sensitive public.[14]

But on the topic of congressional reform, as in many other
matters, Representatives' views are not simply reflections of elec-

[14] Also relevant is the finding that members who accept the notion that a
Representative ought to work for what his constituents want, rather than for
his own personal views, were more favorable toward reform than were those
who disagreed with that notion. Thus (to use Heinz Eulau's terms) the
"instructed delegates" were more inclined toward reform than were the
Burkean "trustees" (see *The Legislative System*, Chap. 12).

toral situations and policy orientations. The manner in which the member defines his role as a Congressman also helps to structure his views toward reform.

The role of Congress envisioned by a member of the House bears a relationship to the member's level of support for reform. Employing the classifications in Table 3.1, we found that those members embracing the literary theory (and its two "Whiggish" variants) gave substantially less support to the list of reform proposals than did those in the literary–executive-force and executive-force categories. Attitudes toward a Congress designed on the party-government theory are also associated with varying levels of support for reform. Forty-seven percent of those scoring low on our measure of the party-government theory supported fewer than 40 percent of the reform proposals. On the other hand, only one of the thirteen members (or eight percent) who gave us an unqualified pro-party response fell into the low reform-support category. We should add that those practicing as well as preaching party government were to be found among the ranks of the reformers. Of those members scoring high (at least 96 percent) on a measure of "party unity" on roll-call voting, only 14 percent were to be found in the group supporting less than 40 percent of the reform items. In contrast, over one half (59 percent) of those with low party-unity scores (below 70 percent) fell in the low reform-support group.[15]

Differences in the purposive-role orientations of the members—that is, the variety of substantive ways in which the job of the legislator was interpreted—did not always lead to noticeable variations in the level of support for the 32 reorganization proposals. However, several patterns are discernable.

Given their traditionalistic orientation to the job of Congressman, the Ritualists were naturally less than enthusiastic over proposed changes in existing arrangements. On the other hand, given their problem-solving focus, the Inventors were overrepresented among those acquiescing to at least 60 percent of the reorganization proposals. However, Inventors were also overrepresented in the group favoring fewer than 40 percent of the reforms. We can explain this peculiarity by recalling our earlier distinction between conservative and liberal Inventors and by reexamining

[15] Party-unity scores were computed by dividing the 88th Congress party-support scores by the sum of the support and opposition scores. This procedure was designed to remove the effect of absences from roll call votes. See *Congressional Quarterly Weekly Report* (October 30, 1964), pp. 2590–2591.

Table 3.6. Conservative Inventors were among those most opposed to reform, whereas liberal Inventors were in the group most enthusiastic for change in House structure and procedures.

As for those few members who were so preoccupied with the problems of being returned at the next election that they could be classified as Opportunists, all fell in the moderate and strong reformist groups. Since the Opportunist wishes to be more visible to his constituents and more powerful in the institution that can provide district-pleasing "loaves and fishes," he looks with favor upon almost any proposal which might reshuffle the existing order in the House.

The foregoing analysis of the relationship between role orientations and attitudes toward reform implies that members least able to act out the roles which they desire to play look with greater favor upon reform proposals than do members whose aspirations are being met by the institution. If the two indicators of satisfaction in Table 3.3 are employed as a measure of the discrepancies between Congress as it is and as it ought to be, this hypothesis is borne out. Members of the House who were classed as "low" on one dimension of satisfaction and either "low" or "moderate" on the other were significantly more supportive of reform than were those Representatives who exhibited a high degree of satisfaction on one dimension and either moderate or high on the second.

But for all the importance of party, constituency characteristics, policy orientation, and perceptions of the functions of Congress and of the individual Congressman, the single most important factor influencing attitudes toward reform is the member's position within the institution itself. Length of continuous service in the House (seniority) appears to be the most obvious and powerful determinant of reformist support or opposition. Table 3.7 indicates how the development of a congressional career, the inculcation of institutional loyalty, and particularly the increasing expectation (or attainment) of power—all concomitants of increasing seniority —work to dampen the enthusiasm for proposed changes in the operations of the House.

Notice that the *expectation* of power is listed as a force leading to opposition to reform; apparently a member need not actually hold one of the coveted committee or subcommittee chairmanships (or equivalent minority-party positions) in order to oppose most reorganization proposals. The opinion-molding effects of long tenure in the House, coupled with the expectation that seniority will

shortly provide a formal leadership position, are evidently sufficient
to make high-seniority members who *do not* hold top committee
positions just as hostile to reform as those members who *do* hold
such positions. Table 3.8 provides evidence for this generalization.
Those Congressmen who have served six to ten terms show the same
level of support for reform whether or not they hold one of the
formal leadership positions.[16] And within both the leader and

TABLE 3.7

Seniority and Support for Reform

Length of Service in the House

Percentage of reform items supported	1 TERM	2–5 TERMS	6–10 TERMS	11 OR MORE TERMS
0–39% (Low)	24%	28%	38%	100%
40–59% (Moderate)	35	39	50	0
60–100% (High)	41	33	13	0
	100%	100%	101%	100%
(Number of respondents)	(17)	(36)	(24)	(9)

nonleader categories, opposition to reform mounts with increasing
seniority. The institutional stakes that make reform unattractive
are especially salient for the senior members of the majority party.
Democratic party leaders, in control of the 88th Congress, were
somewhat more opposed to change than their Republican counterparts.

It might be argued, of course, that the reformist bias of low-
seniority members results not from their status as newcomers but
from other factors which may be related to low seniority. These
members, for example, come disproportionately from districts that
generate the kinds of pressures identified in our earlier analysis

[16] Those members designated as formal House ''leaders'' include respondents holding one or more of the following positions in the 88th Congress:
legislative and Appropriations Committee chairmen and ranking minority
members; chairmen and ranking minority members of the subcommittees of
the Appropriations Committee; the Speaker, Majority Leader, and Majority
Whip; and the Minority Leader, Minority Whip, and the Republican
Conference Chairman.

with high support for reform. And in like fashion, Congressmen most insulated from demanding constituencies and electoral uncertainties are precisely those members most likely to acquire high seniority.

Seniority, it must be conceded, is not unrelated to some of the other variables that we have found to be correlated with support for reform. A noticeable relationship exists between a number of

TABLE 3.8

Seniority, Formal Leadership Position, and Support for Reform*

	SENIORITY			
	6–10 Terms		11 or More Terms	
Percentage of reform items supported	*Non-leaders*	*Leaders***	*Non-leaders*	*Leaders***
0–39% (Low)	41%	41%	100%	79%
40–59% (Moderate)	41	41	0	16
60–100% (High)	18	18	0	5
	100%	100%	100%	100%
(Number of respondents)	(17)	(17)	(3)	(19)

* In order that we might have enough cases for quantitative analysis, we combined our general-sample respondents (with six or more terms in the House) with our special oversample of House leaders. (See Appendix A for an explanation of this leadership oversample.) This procedure in no way affects the validity of the findings.

** See footnote 16 for our definition of formal House leaders.

characteristics of congressional districts and the seniority of their Representatives. For example, Southern districts tend to be rural and one-party rather than urban and competitive, and Representatives from these districts have greater average seniority than do members from other types of constituencies. Further, these same Southern members are likely to exhibit the kind of policy and ideological orientation (a high degree of support for the "conservative coalition") that is so strongly associated with opposition to reform.

To continue with this example, what is it that motivates the "typical" Southern member to oppose most of the reform proposals on our list? Is it because he is Southern? Because he is likely to represent a rural or mixed—rather than an urban—district? Because he has little competition in the general election? Is it the result of his higher than average conservatism? His Ritualist role orientation? His "Whiggish" theory of Congress? His relative satisfaction with the existing order in the House?

TABLE 3.9

Seniority, Support for "Conservative Coalition," and
Support for Reform

SENIORITY

	Low (1–5 terms)			High (6 or more terms)		
	"Conservative Coalition" Support*			"Conservative Coalition" Support*		
Percentage of reform items supported	0–19% (Low)	20–79% (Moderate)	80–100% (High)	0–19% (Low)	20–79% (Moderate)	80–100% (High)
0–39% (Low)	5%	37%	40%	17%	50%	73%
40–59% (Moderate)	32	42	40	67	33	27
60–100% (High)	63	21	20	17	17	0
	100%	100%	100%	101%	100%	100%
(Number of respondents)	(19)	(19)	(15)	(6)	(12)	(15)

* See footnote 13 for a definition of "conservative coalition" support.

These questions are difficult to answer with certainty because all of these characteristics tend to go together. But to the extent that we have been able to "push" our data, the answer is that *all* of the characteristics of members and their districts make an independent contribution, however small, to attitudes toward reform.[17] To take but two of these variables, Table 3.9 indicates that *both* increasing seniority *and* a high level of support for a conservative policy position are independently associated with opposition to reform. This multiplicity of factors explains why the influence of

[17] The limited size of our sample made it difficult to undertake the kind of multivariate analysis that would permit us to measure the impact of each factor upon reform support independent of every other possible factor.

seniority is not more pervasive than it is. There are "class traitors" at both ends of the reform spectrum. Many junior members are hostile to the bulk of the reorganization proposals, and a number of senior Congressmen support a high proportion of the reform items. The inconsistency of the "class traitor" can further be explained if one recalls that not all of the 32 reform proposals that make up our measure of reformism are of the same type. Some, for example, would move Congress in the direction of one theory, some in the direction of another. There is, in fact, something for everyone on the list of reforms.

Thus no single factor is likely to explain the level of support given to reformism by any single member of the House. The high seniority "class traitors," who support a large number of reforms, may be deserting their senior colleagues, but also they may be loyal to their fellow liberals, urbanites, or Inventors. A first-term Representative may support his fellow freshmen by accepting certain reforms but may desert his seniority "class" and oppose other reforms because he is a Southerner or a conservative or a Ritualist.

Congressional Reformism Is Different

In summarizing the foregoing discussion, we find most striking the rather sharp divergence in goals between reformists *inside* and *outside* Congress. These differences are often obscured by the use of a common terminology. Almost everyone speaks of "strengthening" Congress. But to the political scientist, who tends to be executive oriented by philosophy and experience; to the Washington journalist, for whom the executive (especially the President) makes better copy than Congress; and to the general public, for whom presidential actions, policies, and presence are the most visible and comprehensible elements of the federal government—to most of these people, "strengthening" Congress means making it more responsive (in extreme cases, even submissive) to executive branch requests. On the other hand, when Congressmen speak of "strengthening" their own institution, they mean many vague and often conflicting things; but with few exceptions they assuredly do *not* mean relegating Congress to a secondary role in the making of government policy.

Can Congress add anything meaningful to policy making if its

approval of executive proposals is a foregone conclusion? Can
strong congressional party organizations be built that will not be
captured by the presidential wings of the two parties? These
questions seem not to have bothered many noncongressional proponents of change, but they guide (and complicate) the philosophies
of those within the House and Senate who are at least partially
dissatisfied with the *status quo* yet are not willing to surrender
their side of the constitutional tug-of-war by which the American
government makes policy.

The divergence between those who call for reform on the outside
and those who work for reform on the inside can also be seen by
examining the low levels of support given to some of the 32 proposed changes in our survey. The least popular proposals among
House members are the very items that most concern the outside
critics. Consider the question of congressional ethics. Only 35
percent of the members assented to the idea of enforcing the
existing rule that a member's salary be reduced in proportion to his
"avoidable" absences from House sessions.[18] As for the matter of
"rationalizing" the fragmented, poorly coordinated appropriations process, only 15 percent of the members of the House in the
88th Congress approved of passing appropriations through a single,
omnibus bill.[19] And on the frequently discussed and critical
question of curbing the automatic operation of the seniority system
in choosing committee chairmen, the most "popular" of three
alternative means of selecting chairmen—election by party caucus
—received support from only 29 percent of the members.[20]

It seems an important question, therefore, why critics *in* Congress and critics *of* Congress are operating on such different wave
lengths. Why, as is apparently the case, does the map of reform look
so different from the perspective within and without Congress?

Finally, many readers may feel disposed to wonder: why not
some reform, at least? We have pointed out a few areas of rather
broad consensus: (1) many Congressmen complain about similar
kinds of problems; (2) among Congressmen there is widespread
dissatisfaction with certain aspects of congressional functioning;
(3) House members are generally agreed that the institution ought
to be built on the literary model, or its Whiggish variant. Moreover,

[18] See Appendix B, Table B-1, proposal 22.
[19] See Appendix B, Table B-1, proposal 31.
[20] See Appendix B, Table B-1, proposal 26.

our research reveals an important handful of reform items that received the assent of a majority of the members. Yet at the end of the 88th Congress (when our survey was completed), none of these proposals had been given favorable action. What was blocking the apparent majority will on these items? Why were so many of the proposed reforms rejected by the members themselves? The answer: a good many things—some trivial, some important. A description of some of these things will occupy us in the following chapter.

4 THE ECONOMY OF CHANGE

Healthy institutions can and must change; for any institution that maintains a stubborn imperviousness to its changing environment risks the dangers of debilitation and obsolescence. Many institutions are able to survive over time by radically changing their work patterns, while still clinging to symbolic elements of their historic past. With these anachronistic symbols an institution may seek to maintain the fiction of changelessness, and thus to resolve the tension between stability and innovation.

As we pointed out, the American Congress has undergone a few rather striking changes during the past few decades: while many of the traditional forms have been retained, certain aspects of congressional operations would now be unrecognizable to legislators of a few generations ago. But, of course, the argument of many congressional reformers—and not confined to those of the executive-force variety—is that Congress has been insufficiently adaptive to the changed policy environment in which it finds itself. A Damoclean sword now hangs over legislatures in many countries: if legislators do not respond to the complex demands made on them, the executives, bureaucrats, judges, and—in some nations—military leaders and mobs will be less hesitant to act. This fact of life constitutes a great justification for serious examination of the politics of congressional reform.[1]

[1] We are indebted to Ralph K. Huitt for his discussion of stability and change in ''Congressional Reorganization: The Next Chapter''

92

Our discussion to this point has been directed toward the attitudinal setting in which congressional innovation takes place. By analyzing the alternative theories of Congress, the role of public opinion, and the attitudes of members themselves, we have tried to characterize the varied facets of the ''congressional image.'' The theme that pervades our findings is the variety of perspectives—values, viewpoints, and interests—that citizens employ in setting goals for their national legislature and in assessing its performance.

As we have noted, this lack of agreement on the appropriate functions of Congress and the Congressman calls into question the relevance of the rational-comprehensive model of change, since consensus on ultimate values is a necessary (although not sufficient) condition for an orderly, rational progression from goals to problems to solutions. If the reform of Congress is simply a question of determining ''how it could do better what it wants to do''[2] then we must understand that neither Congressmen nor the public is agreed on what Congress ought to do.

It is in light of this lack of agreement that Congressmen must decide whether to expend their resources in identifying themselves with certain innovations in congressional procedures, much less with reformism in general. No politician can devote his time, energy, and influence to every goal on his personal or political agenda. Every ''expenditure'' of these precious resources must be carefully calculated—a process not unfamiliar to politicians elected to the national legislature.[3] In the field of congressional reorganization, the costs of purposeful action can be high when the goals sought are sharply disputed. The politics of reform is therefore a question of priorities.

The quandary of the individual Congressman, writ large, is the problem of constructing a viable coalition for reform action. It is to this topic—the processes of mobilizing support for change—that we must now turn. If there is little agreement on ultimate goals, how does innovation come about? Why is there not more of it? Why is there as much as there is? In this chapter, we will explore some of

---

(a paper presented at the annual meeting of the American Political Science Association, Chicago, Ill., September 8–12, 1964), pp. 4ff.

[2] This orientation to reform was suggested on ''Congress Needs Help'' (NBC Television News Special, November 24, 1965).

[3] The reader is referred to the model of political action set forth in Richard Neustadt, *Presidential Power* (New York: John Wiley, 1960).

the deterrents to reformist coalitions, by referring to specific examples that emerged from our interviews. Some successful strategies of reformist coalition building will also be identified; and in Chapter 5 we will demonstrate how these strategies operated in the 89th Congress (1965–1966).

Forces for Stability

Established institutions build up an impressive resistance to change—in part because there is a great attraction to settled ways of doing things. Of course, the structural "givens" of an institution are far from neutral in their effects upon the participants and upon policy making: by limiting the acceptable range of behaviors, these "givens" foster the goals of some persons and interests and frustrate the goals of others. But, congressional rules and procedures remain relatively stable presumably because they manage to satisfy sufficient numbers of members and interests who are strong enough to preserve them. And the longer these procedures survive, the more they tend to be venerated as the bequests of wise and honored forebears. Indeed, constant structural turmoil would be viewed by most observers as *prima facie* evidence that the institution was unable to cope with the conflicting demands converging upon it.

As we have observed, reformism does not seem to be the dominant mood of the House. Few items in our list of 32 proposals managed to command majority support; those items that were supported by a majority were not effected during the time period in which our survey was conducted. And, as for assessing the probable chances for adoption of any of the 32 proposals, our respondents were even more cautious: only five of the 32 reforms were judged to have at least an even chance of adoption within the succeeding 10 years. Powerful forces must be reinforcing the status quo. What are these forces? Why should members consider reformism a hazardous and unproductive commitment?

TWO "UNSOLVABLE" PROBLEMS

The majority of the problems that burden Congressmen lie outside the scope of traditional reform alternatives. These problems include the normal vicissitudes of electoral politics, the moral dilemmas political men face in resolving the pressures which converge on them, and the staggering difficulties of making informed choices in a complex world. Our interviews indicated that these larger problems were those that seemed most relevant to members as they reflected upon the objectives that they had set for themselves. In fact, these problems accounted for all but about 20 percent of the "complaints" voiced by our respondents. The remainder consisted of less encompassing irritants such as the seniority system, committee operations, and rules and procedures.

Many of the larger problems are inherent in the contemporary role of the democratic politician. They may be somewhat alleviated by specific reforms but never removed. "Probably the problem of the modern legislature cannot be solved," Dahl and Lindblom write —although, they add, it might be reduced by adopting certain reforms.[4]

Complex decision making. A conventional but limited remedy for many informational and decision-making problems is "more staff assistance."[5] While Congressmen differ in their inclinations to utilize additional staff help, most are agreed that larger staffs are both desirable and inevitable. A large majority (83 percent) of our sample favored increasing each Representative's clerk-hire allowance to permit the hiring of an Administrative Assistant in accordance with Senate practice.[6] On the other hand, large staffs simply do not complement the operating styles of some members; nor do staff resources, however numerous or capable, actually remove the dilemma of decision making in a complex world. Not even the President, with the support of nearly two and one-half million federal employees, is able to avoid this dilemma.

Electoral vulnerability. Another type of problem, largely beyond the members' power to remedy, derives from the strains resultant of a democratic electoral system and its campaigns and elections. Nearly 40 percent of our respondents mentioned electoral vulnerability—the need to court constituents and to engage in constant

---

[4] Robert A. Dahl and Charles E. Lindblom, *Politics, Economics, and Welfare* New York: Harper and Row, 1953), pp. 322–323.

[5] For a general study of congressional staffing, see Kenneth Kofmehl, *Professional Staffs of Congress* (West Lafayette, Ind.: Purdue University Studies, 1962).

[6] See Appendix B, Table B–1, proposal 2.

TABLE 4.1

Competitiveness of District and Frequency of Member Complaints
about Electoral Problems

	COMPETITIVENESS OF DISTRICT*	
	"Marginal" districts	*"Safe"* districts
Mentioned one or more personal electoral problems**	48%	31%
Failed to mention personal electoral problems	52	69
	100%	100%
(Number of respondents)	(33)	(54)

* "Marginal" districts are defined as those in which the respondent received less than 60 percent of the vote in the November 1962 congressional election. "Safe" districts are those in which the member polled 60 percent or more of the vote.

** "Personal electoral problems" include complaints about the frequency of elections, constant campaigning, physical distance between Washington and the district, electoral vulnerability, and the necessity of considering constituent policy preferences in order to assure reelection.

campaigning—as impinging on their personal performances as Congressmen. Legislators who come from competitive two-party districts naturally perceive these problems with particular apprehension. Their more fortunate colleagues from "safe" districts regard electoral hazards with somewhat more equanimity. Table 4.1 contrasts the frequency with which personal electoral problems were mentioned by Congressmen from "marginal" districts and by members from more secure districts.

One means of alleviating the strain of constant campaigning and frequent elections is the proposal to increase terms in the House of Representatives to four years. Proposed constitutional amendments providing four-year terms for Representatives have languished in House and Senate committees for some time.[7] The idea gained unexpected new impetus when President Johnson, in his 1966 State of the Union message, announced his support and urged "swift action":

> The present two-year term requires most members . . . to divert enormous energies to an almost constant process of campaign-

[7] See, for example, *Joint Committee Hearings* (1965), Part 4, pp. 691–696; and Part 10, pp. 1522ff.

ing, depriving this nation of the fullest measure of both their skill and their wisdom. Today, too, the work of government is far more complex than in our early years, requiring more time to learn and more time to master the technical tasks of legislating. And a longer term will serve to attract more men of the highest quality to political life. The nation, the principle of democracy, and I think each congressional district, will all be better served by a four-year term. . . .[8]

The President's timetable called for the new system to become operative after 1972.

The arguments in favor of the proposal are straightforward. The two-year electoral cycle is criticized as excessively expensive and time-consuming. Moreover, it probably intensifies the localism in the House, since, the moment they take their seats, many members must start preparing for the next primary or the next general election. A longer interval between elections, it is argued, would allow Representatives to devote more time during each term to their House duties, however these duties might be defined. Advocates of the present system maintain that members ought to have the maximum contact with their constituents and that frequent election campaigns reinforce legitimate constituent demands upon a member.

If the choice were left to a vote of the House, the four-year term would have a good chance of adoption: two thirds of our respondents backed such a proposal.[9] A major complicating factor, of course, is that the process of a constitutional amendment requires the assent of other political actors. The normal procedure for amending the Constitution—approval by two thirds of both houses of Congress and ratification by three fourths of the states—is at best a task of calculated difficulty. On this question in particular, Senators are unlikely to share the enthusiasm of their House colleagues. The political mathematics of a six-year term for Senators and a four-year term for Representatives would mean that the latter would enjoy a "free shot" at a Senate seat in an average of one out of two senatorial elections—thus, when a senatorial election occurred at the midpoint of a Congressman's term, the Congressman could run for the Senate seat and, if defeated, continue to serve in the House. A possible answer to Senate objections would be

[8] *Congressional Record*, 89th Congress, 2nd session (January 12, 1966, daily edition), p. 131.

[9] See Appendix B, Table B–1, proposal 7.

a provision requiring members to resign from the House before campaigning for the Senate.

Prior to President Johnson's endorsement, the four-year term was but a remote possibility because of the anticipated constitutional difficulties and because of Senate objections. Furthermore, within the House itself, the opponents of the measure (though a minority of 33 percent) were very strongly committed to their position: more than eight out of ten in this group were willing to play an active role in opposing the proposal.[10] These barriers to the extension of the terms of Representatives were reflected in the pessimistic estimates of the likelihood of House passage of such a reform. In contrast to the 68 percent vote of approval for the measure, nearly 80 percent of the respondents felt the measure had less than an equal chance of adoption within the next decade.

THE CONGRESSIONAL POWER STRUCTURE

Other reform problems are difficult to resolve because they flow from the existing power structure of Congress. The most pervasive damper on reformist thought and action is the known hostility of the seniority and elective leadership in Congress to many crucial kinds of changes. Naturally enough, these leaders are sensitive to direct threats to their own prerogatives—threats which are indeed implied by many of the most far-reaching reform proposals. The seven least favored proposals (rejected by between 71 and 86 percent of the respondents) are all concerned with the principal features of the congressional hierarchy—committee membership and prerogatives, and the seniority system.[11]

Younger members quickly learn the costs of challenging the prerogatives of the House leadership. The very factors that induce the young Congressman to respond positively to proposed changes —namely, political insecurity and low status within the House— create at the same time strong deterrents to a concrete challenge of the status quo.

Even before the newly elected member sets foot in the Capitol, he receives evidences of the value of good relations with the ''congressional establishment.'' The first congratulatory letter from his party leaders puts the freshman member on double notice: he is to

---

[10] See Appendix B, Table B–1, proposal 7.
[11] See Appendix B, Table B–1, proposals 26–32.

become a member of a legislative body rich in tradition, and he is a representative of one of the two great national parties. This notice subtly suggests that established patterns are not to be criticized or rejected incautiously. Very early in his House career, the freshman is asked to state his preferences in committee assignments—an early reminder that those who have acquired high status in Congress have the power to alter significantly his legislative life. Good committee assignments, favorable disposition of his bills, expeditious handling of projects for his district, liberal contributions from his party's Congressional Campaign Committee, even a pleasant office suite— these and other of the member's desires can be facilitated by friendly leaders, thwarted by hostile ones. Only the strongly disaffected or the "professional maverick" will mount a persistent campaign against those who guard the ramparts of legislative power. This is the import of Speaker Sam Rayburn's famous advice to his younger colleagues: "If you want to *get* along, *go* along."

Low seniority members are particularly vulnerable to intrahouse pressures for yet another reason. In their first few terms, Congress-men must devote much attention to digesting the congressional "folkways" and developing expertise in committee work. (Among our respondents who mentioned "learning the ropes" as a pressing problem, two thirds were in their first term.) Members who look forward to a productive career on Capitol Hill soon learn the importance of developing a policy specialty, preferably within their committee assignment, and of "doing their homework." As Speaker Rayburn once remarked, "It takes awhile for a man to learn, and get established, and gain his full influence. He doesn't reach his full usefulness in his first term or two."[12] Any deviation from this general pattern of compliance and specialization would thus be quite costly in terms of energies diverted to a challenge of the power structure.

It is true that congressional folkways provide the individual member with considerable latitude in casting his votes. Even on important issues, he may often bolt his party leadership without fear of sanctions by using the protective camouflage of "voting his district." Yet district fealty can seldom be applied to matters of rules and procedures, which have at best only a tangential interest to the voters back home.

---

[12] Quoted in Booth Mooney, *Mr. Speaker* (Chicago: Follette Publishing Company, 1964), p. 166.

Young Turks and old fogies. The enormous barriers to reform of the seniority structure are demonstrated by an inspection of the reactions to the four proposals for modifying seniority, which were among our list of 32 items. Table 4.2 reaffirms our earlier finding that the seniority leaders themselves are the most vigorous op-

TABLE 4.2

Seniority and Support for Changes in the Seniority System

	SENIORITY	
	Low (1–5 terms)	High (6 or more terms)
Proposal	*Percent supporting*	*Percent supporting*
Require members to forfeit seniority privileges after each six consecutive terms.	18%	6%
Continue the present system of selecting committee chairmen by seniority, but permit no member to serve as chairman in more than one out of three Congresses.	21	10
Select the chairman of each committee by vote of the majority-party members of the committee.	35	0
Select committee chairmen for each Congress from the three senior (majority) members of each committee and by means of the party caucus.	44	6
(Number of respondents)	(53)	(34)

ponents of any modification of the current distribution of power. The pessimism that surrounds these proposals for fundamental alterations of Congress stems from the simple fact that those who are most likely to be dissatisfied are also those with the least influence and that those with the most influence have nothing to gain by changing the status quo. This attitude is reflected by the familiar quip that is attributed to a number of senior Representatives and Senators: "When I first arrived in Congress, I hated the seniority system. But the longer I'm here, the better I like it."

Self-interest is not the only attitude supporting the present system. One viewpoint—expressed frequently by Ritualists—suggests that the seniority system counts for very little aside from the selection of committee and subcommittee chairmen (and not even all of the latter). "What counts is who works," one Congressman told us. Defenders of seniority also stress the necessity of experience among those who lead the committees and bear the brunt of negotiations with executive-branch officials. In this view, occasional incompetence or senility is a tolerable price to pay for this valuable experience. Supporters of the seniority system say that it, like democracy itself (in Winston Churchill's famous aphorism), is the worst of systems—except for all the others. Both Republican and Democratic Congressmen contemplate with genuine fear a nonautomatic selection system that would produce conflict, haggling, ill-feeling, and a divisive effect on the two parties and on Congress itself.

Finally, the defenders of seniority point out that the system also has an intangible but salutary impact upon legislative-executive relations. The influence of Congress is enhanced, they argue, because seniority leaders represent "immovable objects" with which the executive branch must contend. As long as committee chairmen are installed more or less for life, the President and his advisors must accept that fact and attempt to bargain with them. Disgruntled executives are not tempted to engage in campaigning in order to elect more compliant chairmen. For this reason, many members who are troubled over the decline of Congress take comfort from the belief that, however irksome a chairman may seem to his colleagues, he may be even more so to executive-branch officials.

None of the alternative methods of selecting committee leaders seems to have generated significant support. Of the dozen or so proposals that have been made with some frequency,[13] four were selected for inclusion in our survey. One alternative is a requirement that Congressmen retire after every sixth consecutive term. They would then have to wait two years before trying for reelection; and if successful, they would begin at the bottom of the seniority list. The version of the proposal employed in our survey was somewhat less drastic, requiring only that members forfeit seniority (but not their congressional seats) after six terms. Only

[13] For a summary of the most popular proposals, see U.S. Congress, Joint Committee on the Organization of the Congress, *Interim Report* (Washington: Government Printing Office, 1965), p. 11.

14 percent of our respondents favored this proposal.[14] In addition
to the usual hostility toward changes in the seniority system,
Congressmen criticize such a measure because it fails to distinguish
between capable and incompetent chairmen and because it would in
no way guarantee that a chairman would be responsible to his
colleagues during the terms he served. It would merely limit the
time period of a member's seniority leadership. Similar objections
are raised against a second alternative, that of "tumbling the
chairmanships." Under this system, the present practice of selecting chairmen on the basis of seniority would be retained, with the
proviso that no member could serve as chairman of his committee
for more than one out of every three Congresses. The chairmanships
would thus be rotated among the more senior members of each
committee. Only 17 percent of our respondents favored this
alternative.[15]

Even those who favor elective chairmanships are in disagreement
over who should do the electing. A proposal for allowing each
committee to elect its own leaders has some appeal, probably
because committee members are generally believed to be the best
judges of who is most competent to lead. This proposal, however, is
unacceptable to party-government advocates, who fear that blocs
might form within the committees to elect chairmen not in accord
with the national party program—that is, "mavericks," or even
representatives of the minority party. Thus, the plan would further
fractionize committee power rather than—as the party-government model dictates—bind the committees more closely to the
majority-party caucus. This proposal received the support of 21
percent of the members interviewed.[16]

The most attractive alternatives, relatively speaking, seem to be
those that link the party-responsibility concept with the selection of
committee chairmen. One proposal calls for a majority-caucus
election of chairmen from among the three senior members of each
committee. Ranking minority members would be elected in a similar
manner by the minority caucus. Twenty-nine percent of our
respondents indicated their approval of such a proposal.[17] One
objection to this plan is that members could not knowledgeably

14 See Appendix B, Table B–1, proposal 32.
15 See Appendix B, Table B–1, proposal 30.
16 See Appendix B, Table B–1, proposal 29.
17 See Appendix B, Table B–1, proposal 26.

evaluate the work of colleagues on committees other than their own. But some members reject this alleged defect by explaining that Congressmen would seek out trusted colleagues—just as they do in casting votes on legislation—in order to learn the qualifications of those eligible for chairmanships.

The committee system is another area in which a relatively high level of member dissatisfaction is unsupported by a consensus on concrete reform proposals. Approximately 30 percent of our respondents complained about one or more of the following elements of the committee system: the power and prerogatives of chairmen, the manner of selecting committee members, the confused and overlapping jurisdictions of committees and subcommittees, or the recruitment and responsibilities of committee staffs. In addition, the performance of particular committees, especially the Committee on Rules, was criticized by a significant minority of the members of the House. Yet only one committee-oriented reform received particularly impressive support—the extremely general proposal to reformulate committee jurisdictions in order to reduce the overlap and to conform more closely with jurisdictional divisions among the executive agencies.[18]

The committee system is generally conceded to have proved an effective method of dividing up the congressional work load. Disputes over committee practices tend to be concentrated upon specific policy controversies. For example, the agitation during the 89th Congress for an easier method of discharging bills from legislative committees revolved around a single measure—District of Columbia home rule—which had long been pigeonholed by the Southern-controlled House District Committee. (Chapter 5 provides a recounting of this controversy.)

Party leaders and followers. Disputes over functions of elective leaders often turn upon differing interpretations of the actual or the desired role of Congress in the governmental process. In regard to the former, for example, there is disagreement over the factual question of how much independent power the majority leadership can wield in facilitating or slowing the passage of legislation. Some observers point out that the leadership must often delay bringing measures to a floor vote in order to construct a majority coalition, and that often only temporary majorities can be fashioned for contentious bills. The necessary processes of ''counting the house,''

[18] See Appendix B, Table B–1, proposal 8.

bargaining, and building consensus demand precise timing and often require delay. The importance of timing in the legislative process is often cited as one justification of the power of the Committee on Rules to regulate the flow of bills to the House floor; but the committee is not always induced to operate as an arm of the leadership.

Disagreements as to the desired role of the leadership in the legislative process turn on questions such as the following. How should power be apportioned between the majority and minority parties? How should power be distributed within the parties? What criteria ought to determine the progress of legislation through the two houses? Should the leadership be empowered or even required to press for a vote on a major piece of legislation a set period after its introduction or a short time after it has been reported from committee? Or should such legislation be held back until a preponderant majority—a near-consensus—is assured?

One general view holds that extensive delays and avoidance of decisions are harmful to Congress and the nation. A requirement for decisions within a "reasonable" time might have a beneficial disciplinary effect upon party and committee leaders. If a major bill were defeated, efforts then could be redirected toward achieving agreement on an alternative version of the measure. Insofar as the present system encourages delay and dispersal of influence, it permits members to avoid individual responsibility by blaming the leadership or the Rules Committee for the failure of Congress to act. To the extent that the system encourages repeated compromises, it produces—as one respondent put it—mere "legislative jelly" rather than a clear-cut resolution of issues.

To this position it is answered that the slow modification of an existing bill is more desirable than trying to build a new coalition after the measure has been defeated. Moreover, an institution that disperses and obscures responsibility has distinct advantages for many of its members, who find it useful to reduce political pressures upon themselves by shifting to others the blame for the success or failure of certain measures. That the House Committee on Rules performs this valuable function is clearly demonstrated by our survey data. The proposal to strip that committee of its blocking and delaying power (permitting it only the so-called "traffic cop" function of setting the terms of debate on the floor) was opposed by a majority of our respondents in the 88th

Congress.[19] Although opposition to this reform was heaviest among the more senior members, a substantial minority of the first-, second-, and third-term Congressmen in our sample were allied with the senior leadership on this matter.

Reform measures that would fashion Congress along the lines of the party-government model, like those that would reconstruct the seniority and committee systems, often flounder because they threaten the existing congressional leadership. Only by minimizing the threat to these leaders could a party-oriented proposal enjoy some chance for success.

One mild party-oriented reform on our list received moderate support: fifty-eight percent of the respondents favored the establishment of party policy committees to develop basic party strategies and legislative priorities.[20] No doubt this proposal benefited from the fact that the House Republicans had already established a policy committee. Until 1965 this group received no formal House appropriations and relied instead upon contributions from the clerk-hire allowances of Republican members of the group.[21] These Representatives encouraged their Democratic colleagues to establish a similar group since they assumed that Democratic action would ensure that House funds would then be provided for both groups. (This in fact occurred during the 89th Congress.) Among the Democratic respondents, many young liberals favored establishment of such a policy committee, but the party leaders were not particularly eager to sponsor an entity that would rival the prerogatives of seniority and leadership.

Other party-oriented innovations did not fare as well as the policy-committee proposal. The guarantee of increased committee staffs for the minority party received the support of a majority (60 percent) of respondents.[22] But more than 60 percent of the *majority* party (Democratic) respondents, including most of the leaders, opposed the minority-staffing proposal. The difficulty of persuading the majority to make concessions to the minority in such matters is well known. Yet the issue remains a live one because of the persistent efforts of a significant group of Republicans. Although the Republican minority will probably not be able to win

[19] See Appendix B, Table B–1, proposal 18.

[20] See Appendix B, Table B–1, proposal 12.

[21] See the discussion in Chapter 5.

[22] See Appendix B, Table B–1, proposal 10.

a formal procedural change incorporating a favorable formula for the distribution of staff personnel, they have in fact been successful in negotiating concessions in individual committees.

CONFLICTING GOALS AND UNCERTAIN SOLUTIONS

Aside from barriers to change inherent in the congressional power structure, the partisan, ideological, and regional differences which cut across many of the great issues of American politics also act as divisive forces in any movements toward reform. Although the advocates and opponents of change typically state their positions in politically neutral terms, it should be clear that very few changes in such an overtly political institution can be considered in a truly neutral way. To curb the filibuster in the Senate, to weaken the House Rules Committee's power to delay legislation, to select chairmen on some basis other than seniority—even though these issues may be debated in terms of grand national goals or traditions, all participants recognize that these proposals have important political consequences for them and for the policies they espouse.

Case: The four-year term. The idea of a four-year term for members of the House is an excellent case in point. As we have pointed out previously, a considerable majority of the House of Representatives would find this innovation to their liking. But this majority is also shrewdly concerned with the effects of such a proposal on legislative-executive relations, the political composition of the House, and the resultant policy decisions of that body. If the four-year terms were coterminous with those of the President, the so-called "coattails" effect might strongly influence the results of the congressional campaigns by liberalizing the House and making it more responsive to presidential leadership.[23] If, on the other hand, elections were held in nonpresidential years, the arrangement might increase congressional independence from the executive and enchance the conservative coloration of the House.

One might presume that the present two-year term would be defended most strenuously by Representatives whom it inconveniences the least—namely, those members from safe constituencies—

[23] See, for example, Charles Press, "Presidential Coattails and Party Cohesion," *Midwest Journal of Political Science*, 7 (November 1963), 320–335.

and that the proposed four-year term would be most strongly
advocated by those whom the present system inconveniences the
most—Representatives from competitive two-party districts. However, our data do not support this common-sense explanation. Table
4.3 indicates that ideology—liberalism or conservatism on legislative policy matters—influenced a considerable portion of the
support of, and opposition to, four-year terms ending in presiden-

TABLE 4.3

Support for "Conservative Coalition," Competitiveness of District,
and Support for Four-Year Terms in the House
of Representatives

"Conservative Coalition" Support*

Position on four-year-term proposal***	0–19% (LOW)		20–79% (MODERATE)		80–100% (HIGH)	
	Competitiveness** Marginal	Safe	Competitiveness Marginal	Safe	Competitiveness Marginal	Safe
SUPPORT	88%	88%	62%	67%	42%	59%
OPPOSE	12	12	38	33	58	41
	100%	100%	100%	100%	100%	100%
(Number of respondents)	(8)	(17)	(13)	(18)	(12)	(17)

* See Chapter 3, footnote 13, for a definition of "Conservative Coalition" sup-
port.
** Marginal and safe districts are defined in a note accompanying Table 4.1.
*** For the exact wording of the four-year-term proposal, see Appendix B,
Table B-1, proposal 7.

tial-election years. It also shows that the marginality of a member's
district made little difference in his attitude toward this proposal—
although as one moves to the right end of the ideological spectrum,
marginal-district members displayed somewhat stronger opposition
to the reform than did their colleagues from safe districts.

Further analysis of the data in Table 4.3 suggests that partisan
voting also determines attitudes toward this reform. Of the 14
Representatives in the "high" conservatism category who opposed
the four-year term, 10 were Republicans. These men would probably suffer most in an era of Democratic ascendancy, because the
probability of their party's becoming the congressional majority
would be lessened, therefore reducing their chances of becoming

committee chairmen. And while virtually all the highly conservative Democrats came from safe districts, nearly two thirds of the
conservative Republicans in our survey represented districts which
were closely contested in the 1962 elections. Not only would their
chairmanships in Congress be jeopardized by a four-year term but
perhaps their seats in the House as well.

The difficulty of coalition building was illustrated by the fate of
the four-year-term proposal in 1966. When President Johnson
indicated his support of the measure, there were several hopeful
signs: surveys (including our own) showed a majority of House
members favoring the plan, and observers reported a favorable
majority in the House Judiciary Committee—which would have to
consider the measure. Also, if applause were any measure, the
President's reference to the four-year term was the portion of his
State of the Union message most enthusiastically received by the
assembled legislators. From the moment the Judiciary Committee
hearings opened in early February, however, the very forces we
have been describing began to erode this potential coalition. For, as
the implications of the proposal came to light, the members'
enthusiasm faded visibly.

This erosion was typified by an incident that occurred when
Attorney General Nicholas de B. Katzenbach appeared before the
committee on behalf of the President's proposal.[24] At one point,
Katzenbach remarked that, if the terms of the President and House
members coincided, "legislative-executive party solidarity" would
be promoted. Whereupon Representative Richard Poff (R-Va.),
who had supported four-year terms (but in staggered years),
exclaimed: "I cannot imagine a better argument for the opposite of
what you are trying to uphold. The function of Congress is to defy
the executive when necessary—to resist conformity and standard-
ization."

Caught in the middle of this ideological gulf was Representative
Frank Chelf (D-Ky.), who had introduced the President's proposal
but whose original bill had called for staggered four-year terms. The
following brief exchange took place:

> POFF: I want to be a helpful ally. Which version are you trying
>   to promote?
> CHELF: I'm going to promote any version that can get out of the
>   committee.

[24] Accounts of this incident are found in *New York Times* (February 16,
1966), p. 18; and *National Observer* (February 21, 1966), p. 2.

If the four-year-term proposal could be said to have breathed its last, it must surely have been at this moment. The participants were unsure of the consequences of their proposals; and when some of the possible consequences were spelled out, they found themselves in fundamental disagreement. The radically different versions of the four-year-term proposal reflected this apparently irreconcilable disagreement.

Case: Several "neutral" issues. Even seemingly neutral issues are sometimes less innocent than they seem. Home rule for the District of Columbia, for example, is often justified as a democratic gesture toward residents of the nation's capital or as a measure of efficiency that would relieve Congress of the burden of governing the city. But the issue touches the interests of a wide variety of groups, including local businessmen fearful of higher taxes and Southern members opposed to giving self-rule to a heavily Negro locality. Or consider the ethical question of whether legislators should publicize their financial interests. Congressional advocates of tighter regulation of such businesses as radio and television outlets and financial institutions naturally view disclosure as an aid to their objectives. To the affected businesses and to those members associated with the businesses, disclosure may represent a form of harassment. Indeed, this reform proposal has an impact upon any business or industry regulated by or doing business with the government.

In other issues of apparent minimal political sensitivity, the diversity of goals which members express probably contributes to the maintenance of the status quo. Congressmen define their own and their institution's functions in diverse and conflicting ways. The Ritualist, who is concerned with adherence to established procedures, will assess reform alternatives rather differently than the Inventor, who is interested primarily in solving problems. Likewise, Brokers and Tribunes may have quite diverse reactions to suggestions for change. A member's style of operation may further separate him from other members even of the same party and ideological inclination.

The powerful connection between reform and politics often creates an aura of distrust that every would-be reformer must labor to overcome. If, for example, a conservative Congressman finds himself in agreement with a liberal on some significant procedural change, his likely reaction would not be one of joy at

finding an unexpected ally but rather suspicion that the proposal
includes hidden advantages for his adversary.

Congressional-reform movements have also been subject to the
periodic cycles of political conflict. When majorities are able to
work their will in Congress, they see little need for procedural
change. When majorities are slender or unstable, the need for
attaining high-priority legislative goals diverts attention from reform efforts. Thus reform-minded Congressmen often find themselves in the dilemma of the old man with the leaky roof: when the
sun was shining, there was no need for repair; when it was raining,
it was too difficult to repair.

In those rare instances where these multiple barriers might be
surmounted, the problem of obtaining agreement on the specific
terms of reform measures remains. Generating support for change
is complicated by the inability of human beings to predict the
results of deliberate actions they may take. The final questions on
which a reformist coalition must find agreement are: What will be
the consequences of this reform action? Will it accomplish what it
is designed to do? And will it lead to any unforeseen and
undesirable consequences? These uncertainties frequently frustrate
the efforts of the reformers.

Two seemingly innocuous procedural questions will illustrate the
problems occasioned by a lack of agreement on goals, as well as by
an inability to calculate the results of specific proposals. The
proposals to permit increased radio and television coverage of
legislative proceedings and to adopt the system used in many state
legislatures of tallying roll-call votes by electronic equipment have
both been endorsed as a means of employing the benefits of modern
technology in the legislative process. The first proposal is justified
on the grounds of stimulating public knowledge and understanding
of legislative proceedings; the latter on grounds of simple efficiency. Whatever their appeal, these proposals proved no less
divisive among our respondents than many reforms which were
more overtly political.

The issue of broadcasting is somewhat different in the two houses.
Neither the House nor the Senate has permitted broadcasting or
televising of floor proceedings with the exception of certain special
joint sessions. A number of members, most notably Senator Jacob
K. Javits (R-N.Y.), have advocated the airing of "great debates"
on the floor of either chamber. The Senate permits radio and
television coverage of committee investigations at the commit-

tee chairman's discretion. But because of Speaker Rayburn's adamant opposition, the House did not follow the Senate's lead and Rayburn's precedent has yet to be overturned. However, Rayburn's successor, Speaker John McCormack (D-Mass.), has not appeared so adamant on the question; and certain influential members, including former Representative Oren Harris (D-Ark.), chairman of the Interstate and Foreign Commerce Committee, have repeatedly introduced resolutions to permit broadcasting and televising of committee sessions.

The proponents of greater media coverage usually insist that it would be an important means of attracting and educating the public in the tasks of government.[25] Many proponents also feel that by lifting restrictions on news coverage, Congress would receive more extensive and favorable news coverage than it now does. This coverage might help to overcome the President's great advantage in mass communications. Some Representatives also believe that the House prohibition puts them in an unfavorable position with their Senate colleagues, who can obtain better press by doing the same kinds of things before a microphone or camera. These considerations led 10 Representatives, members of the House Republican Task Force on Congressional Reform and Minority Staffing, to introduce in early 1966 a resolution permitting live radio and television coverage of floor and committee sessions.[26]

Opponents of expanded coverage fear that it might bring out the worst in many of their colleagues. The temptation to grab the limelight and play for the home·audience would, they argue, make a mockery of orderly legislative processes, encourage the tendency to place unfriendly witnesses on trial before the cameras, and turn floor debate into meaningless rhetorical displays. Speaker Rayburn expressed this sentiment:

> When a man has to run for re-election every two years, the temptation to make headlines is strong enough without giving him a chance to become an actor on television. The normal processes toward good law are not even dramatic let alone sensational enough to be aired across the land.[27]

[25] For materials relating to these proposals, see *Joint Committee Hearings* (1965), Part 6, pp. 912–936.

[26] H. Res. 641 (floor sessions) and H. Res. 651 (committee sessions). See *Congressional Record*, 89th Congress, 2nd session (January 12, 1966, daily edition), pp. 109–110.

[27] Cited in Mooney, p. 167.

And one Congressman, interviewed shortly after President Kennedy's assassination, expressed a bitter view of this proposal: "Televise Congress? Do you know what that would mean? Look what happened when they laid that poor devil in the [Capitol] rotunda. Everybody tried to get in the front row to make sure of being on camera."

The item proposed in our survey—a modest suggestion to permit radio and television coverage of House committee proceedings— received the support of a majority (58 percent) of our respondents.[28] But opinions were sharply polarized on this issue: although 26 percent were "strongly for" the proposal, a sizable group of opponents anticipated that they would take more than a nominal position against the measure. Thirty percent of our sample said that they would "talk," "work," or "lead the fight"—as well as simply vote—against the media coverage reform if it came up. (This was the most intense opposition expressed against any of the reforms that received majority assent in our study.) Thus, this proposal is hampered by an insufficient agreement on goals, as well as an inability to calculate which goals would be served by implementing it.

The suggestion to tabulate roll-call votes by electronic means, though somewhat less popular, was equally evocative of intense feelings. Efficiency-minded members looked to electronic voting as a means of saving at least an hour of their time each legislative day. But other members, equally concerned with the demands on their time, predicted quite different results for this reform. They pointed out that in many state legislatures electronic voting has resulted in more frequent roll calls. Some opposing members were also concerned that the voting key might be used by unauthorized persons such as other legislators or even staff aides. Perhaps the chief objection to electronic voting is the resultant elimination of a valuable informal method of exchanging information on the matter being voted upon. A number of members pointed out that the 40 minutes or so required for a roll-call vote is hardly wasted time since it permits them to come to the floor from their offices or committee rooms (or even from downtown Washington), consult with colleagues who are knowledgeable on the issue, check to see how others are voting, and incidentally engage in a little socializing. Since busy Congressmen must spend most of their time away

[28] See Appendix B, Table B–1, proposal 11.

from the floor, the time consumed by a roll call provides an excellent opportunity for this exchange of information.

The seemingly harmless proposal for electronic voting received support from only 41 percent of our respondents; and more than two out of three of those against the measure considered themselves "strongly opposed."[29] In keeping with the general characteristics of their role, Ritualists registered the greatest opposition to the proposal. Almost every opponent of electronic voting expounded his own version of the unintended consequences of this proposal; indeed, perhaps no item in the survey questionnaire so clearly illustrated the hazards of forecasting the results of innovation.

Forces for Change

For all of its stability, Congress is not a static institution. Recent congressional history is marked by numerous, if oftentimes marginal, changes. The attitudinal patterns that emerged from our interviews with Congressmen suggested a few general conditions under which the many obstacles to change may be overcome.

CORNERSTONES OF REFORMIST COALITION BUILDING

Implementing the literary theory. Congressmen place much stock in the need to compete effectively with the executive branch. Presumably reforms that are advocated as potential contributions to Congress' influence would have at least a fighting chance for approval. Indeed, three items dealing with congressional-executive relations received strong support among our respondents.

A proposal to increase the investigative and supervisory powers of the General Accounting Office (designed to function as a congressional watchdog over executive spending) proved to be the most popular item in our list of reform proposals.[30] It was approved by 86 percent of the respondents, although 54 percent judged it to have less than an even chance of adoption in the next decade. The support for this proposal no doubt derives from the widespread feeling among Congressmen that they do not have adequate control over the disposition of appropriated funds. The suggestion for a

[29] See Appendix B, Table B-1, proposal 19.
[30] See Appendix B, Table B-1, proposal 1.

joint congressional committee "to give broad consideration and direction to federal spending" also received high support (73 percent).[31] And it is instructive to note that several related devices, such as informal clearance and veto of executive actions or expenditures, have increasingly come to be employed by congressional committees in recent years to enforce controls on the executive branch.[32]

Another measure designed to give weight to Congress in its struggles with the executive was the proposal to allow the House to require executive officers to furnish, under specified conditions, information requested by any committee.[33] This measure was likewise given little chance of adoption in the immediate future, but it received the approval of 60 percent of the respondents. While some advances have been achieved in obtaining "freedom of information" in specific areas, such as foreign aid, the general problem remains an irritant that Congressmen acknowledge is likely to continue.[34]

One change in the realm of congressional-executive relations which did not meet with high favor was the proposal for "question periods" during which cabinet-rank officials would appear before the entire House to answer queries. While this change is nominally intended to allow more effective congressional oversight, the consensus seemed to be that other less desirable results would come from a question period. One objection held that the proposal represented an indiscriminate grafting from the parliamentary form of government onto the separation-of-powers system. Because executive and legislative officials are not bound by the same party loyalties, their exchanges might degenerate into disorganized squabbling, in which each branch struggled to "make points" over the other. Many members also argued that present congressional

[31] See Appendix B, Table B-1, proposal 5.

[32] On this subject, see Joseph P. Harris, *Congressional Control of Administration* (Washington: The Brookings Institution, 1964), and John S. Saloma, *The Responsible Use of Power* (Washington: American Enterprise Institute, 1964).

[33] See Appendix B, Table B-1, proposal 9.

[34] For a discussion of this problem from the "congressional" perspective, see Charles R. Dechert, *Availability of Information for Congressional Operations* (Washington: American Enterprise Institute, 1966). The activities of the Special Subcommittee on Governmental Information of the House Committee on Government Operations, headed by Representative John E. Moss (D-Calif.), are also symbolic of the concern of many members over the problem of obtaining adequate information from the executive.

committee hearings provide an opportunity for flexible and meaningful questioning and give-and-take between legislators and executive officials. Not only is a question period not needed, they say, but also it would be markedly inferior to present practice.

The field of congressional-executive relations may constitute fertile ground for future reform efforts. This would be true for reasons quite apart from intralegislative politics; for, it is in relation to the powers of the executive that Congress is most in jeopardy. The more meaningful congressional innovations are likely to be those that enhance congressional capabilities for dealing with the executive branch since this variety of reformism begins from goal premises which are widely shared among legislators of both parties and of many ideological and policy dispositions.

Promoting efficiency. Legislators need not always reach agreement on the proper role of Congress before they consider steps designed to increase access to necessary information, expedite the work of their office and committee staffs, or generally render their life on Capitol Hill a bit more tolerable. James Burnham observed that "Quite apart from the theories about the proper place of the legislature, a change would be an improvement if through it Congress were enabled to do better whatever it might be that it was in fact doing.[35]

Apparently this philosophy guided a bipartisan congressional study group that met periodically during the early 1960s to discuss broad problems of congressional change. This group, which included Congressmen from all ranges of the ideological spectrum, was chaired jointly by Representatives Chet Holifield (D-Calif.) and Thomas B. Curtis (R-Mo.).[36] One working paper prepared by the group stressed the intention to point out areas of reform that would "increase efficiency, expedite the business of the House, streamline its functions to meet present-day demands, and otherwise improve the operation of the legislative branch of the federal government." As will be seen in the following chapter, an efficiency motif also characterizes the approach of Senator A. S. Mike Monroney (D-Okla.), who spearheaded the drive for creation of the second Joint Committee on the Organization of the Congress.

We have already suggested that the use of such a politically

---

[35] James Burnham, *Congress and the American Tradition* (Chicago: Henry Regnery, 1959), p. 271.

[36] This study group is discussed briefly in Chapter 5.

neutral word as "efficiency" may in fact conceal sharp differences in policy or ideology. But limited agreement within such an abstract concept can occasionally yield fruitful results. Specific reforms of this *genre* are clearly most likely to win approval if they are linked closely to unrealized personal goals which members consider important. The Legislative Reorganization Act of 1946 gained passage as much for its sugarcoating of a badly needed pay raise as for its abstract appeals to efficiency. Through an adroit political compromise, the bill was able to combine personal and "public" interest. Similarly, the notion of installing a bevy of high-speed computers on Capitol Hill may have some abstract appeal, but it will be more likely to gain support if members can be shown precisely what computers could do to facilitate their personal, political, and legislative tasks.[37]

Our survey indicates that at least several efficiency-oriented reforms show considerable promise of winning approval. For example, we have noted the widespread support (83 percent) for increasing each member's clerk-hire allowance to enable the hiring of an Administrative Assistant. This proposal has a many-faceted appeal: to the extent that he is capable of using staff help at all, a member can direct his added staff toward any purpose he desires. Regardless of his political goals, he may use his aides for research purposes or to lobby for or against legislative proposals. Or he may use added staff to handle constituent matters, to generate publicity, to help prepare for electoral contests, or simply to increase his stock of patronage. (It should be noted, also, that such proposals are not politically neutral; for they clearly enhance the advantages which incumbents enjoy over their nonincumbent challengers—advantages that incumbents are not likely to find objectionable.)

Some members are undoubtedly reluctant to advocate substantial increases in staff or information-processing equipment for fear of offending the taxpayers. "If I could sell people on the idea of doubling my staff," Senator Everett M. Dirksen (R-Ill.) remarked, "I would do it tomorrow."[38]

[37] One very obvious and appealing use of modern electronic equipment would be to computerize members' mailing lists, thus reducing this onerous staff chore (and probably increasing the volume of mass mailings to constituents). On other applications of data storage and retrieval devices, see Kenneth Janda, *Information Systems for Congress* (Washington: American Enterprise Institute, 1965).

[38] On "Congress Needs Help" (NBC Television News Special, November 24, 1965). Actually, the total number of employees for the legislative branch

Although the proposal for hiring Administrative Assistants had not been adopted at this writing, there was a substantial increase in personal staff allowances during the 88th Congress and many Representatives informally designated one key staff member as their Administrative Assistant. The House also authorized additional allowances for college-age summer interns in each member's office. Introduced by Representative John Brademas (D-Ind.), the measure (H. Res. 416) was reported out by the House Committee on Administration on June 16 and was passed the same day.[39] This bill illustrates the combination of virtues needed for successful reform: it provided additional help for understaffed offices during the busy summer months, and it enabled members to encourage goodwill in their districts by satisfying the increasing requests from college students who want to spend a summer working in a congressional office.

Two scheduling changes, which conformed to the general definition of efficiency, also received endorsement from our respondents. Approximately three fourths of the members interviewed were in favor of holding year-long sessions with specified recesses and formally designated days for floor business and for committee business. (The time provided for floor activity would increase as the session proceeded.)[40] This desire for a more orderly allocation of time arises from countless personal and political hardships suffered by Congressmen under the present system. Members were highly desirous of an arrangement whereby they could anticipate having substantial blocks of time available for trips to their districts. And they felt that time could be more effectively allocated on Capitol Hill under a system which takes account of the normal cycle of legislative business—in which committee work tends to be concentrated in the early months of the session and floor debate in the latter months. (Under present House rules, unanimous consent is required before a committee can meet while the House is in session.)

----

has fallen somewhat since passage of the Legislative Reorganization Act of 1946—from 27,946 in 1946 to 25,037 in 1965 (U.S. Civil Service Commission figures as of May 31, 1965).

[39] H. Rept. 523. The House Administration Committee set regulations requiring that interns serve in the Washington offices of Congressmen rather than in their home districts, and that no more than two could be hired in any summer by a Representative. For voting on the measure, see *Congressional Record*, 89th Congress, 1st session (June 16, 1965, daily edition), p. 13312.

[40] See Appendix B, Table B–1, proposals 4 and 6.

The scheduling changes would be relatively noncontroversial for incumbents because they would be allowed more freedom in allocating their time. And the added advantage of these two reforms is that they could be effected by an informal agreement among the party leaders without a formal alteration of the rules.

An advocate of congressional reform must keep in mind that institutions which attempt to build consensus out of striking philosophical and practical conflicts must frequently engage in a certain amount of "inefficient" behavior in order to minimize the level of conflict and resolve the important needs of individual members.[41] At least it would be misleading to expect a collectivity of political bargainers to utilize all the procedures appropriate to the bureaucratic structure of a governmental agency or the hierarchy of a large business firm. One need not be marked as an enemy of efficiency to understand the insight in a remark by Speaker Rayburn, which was related by Treasury Under Secretary Joseph W. Barr, who served in Congress in 1959–1960. Barr tells of bombarding the late Speaker with a series of analytical questions concerning congressional operations until Rayburn exclaimed in exasperation: "Joe, I am worried about you. You seem to have an orderly mind—and this is a disorderly body."[42]

One example of the deceptiveness of efficiency has already been noted in our discussion of electronic voting devices. Another example is provided by the seemingly capricious editorial policies of the *Congressional Record*, the official journal of House and Senate proceedings. Congressmen and Senators are free to modify in any fashion the portion of the journal that records their own speeches or debates. Someone once said that Congressmen are the only people in the world who can think, "I wish I'd said that"— and then say it.

For all the criticism of the practice of "revising and extending" remarks, however, Congressmen remain notably unenthusiastic about the prospect of relinquishing their control over the *Record*: 60 percent of the members interviewed, in fact, opposed this proposal.[43] In support of current practices, it is argued that many

[41] The conflict-reduction functions of senatorial "folkways" provide the theme for Donald R. Matthews' discussion in his *U.S. Senators and Their World* (Chapel Hill: University of North Carolina Press, 1960), Chapter 5.

[42] "The U.S. Congress—A Personal View," an address before the American Society for Public Administration, Washington, D.C., September 22, 1965.

[43] See Appendix B, Table B–1, proposal 20.

junior members, and those members not serving on committees dealing with policies that interest them, have virtually no chance to contribute to the formal debates. By inserting prepared material into the *Record,* they may publicize their views to colleagues and constituents.

Moreover, many members are doubtful of the accuracy of the official reporters, who work in shifts to take down debate in shorthand. One Representative recalled a floor speech in which he criticized federally supported public libraries. "We're becoming modern-day Carnegies," he said, referring to the philanthropic activities of the famous industrialist. However, when the text of his remarks arrived that evening for review, he was quoted as saying, "We're becoming modern Dale Carnegies." It is often alleged that the *Congressional Record* means very little; but for an elected official such misquotations—or the dubious remarks that he may utter in haste—may come back to haunt him in the future. It is not likely, therefore, that members will relinquish their right to shape the *Record* according to their purposes.

STRATEGIES OF INNOVATION

The theme for our discussion of the factors that facilitate and deter congressional change might be paraphrased by referring to Samuel Johnson's comment on how a dog walks on its hind legs: Don't be critical of how well it does; just be amazed that it does it at all. We have surveyed what must appear a formidable array of obstacles to the reform of Congress. The forces that divide members often seem much more powerful than the forces that unite them.

Constituent demands, differences of party, regional loyalties, philosophical attitudes, and even differing personal styles—all of these factors are hazards to coalition building. And then the life expectancy of most coalitions is relatively brief. To gain agreement on the directions which reform should take, not to mention specific reform alternatives, is exceedingly difficult. Considering this difficulty, Dahl and Lindblom concluded that "one major limit to effective reorganization of the American Congress to meet its modern tasks is the extent to which bargaining is built into the American political system . . ."[44]

Substantial amounts of time, energy, and political "credit" must

[44] Dahl and Lindblom, p. 322.

be expended in obtaining agreement on every innovation even slightly controversial. Our discussion has emphasized that most reform issues are controversial in the extreme. These issues will require intense and sustained treatment if they are to be pushed through the legislative mill. Because they are beset with other questions that demand immediate resolution, Congressmen must usually defer action on reform items no matter how desirable the changes may seem. When we observe that Congressmen avoid acting upon reform proposals, we are not criticizing their energy or their courage but merely pointing out that they are unavoidably preoccupied with day-to-day problems and political issues.

The normal problems of coalition building are compounded in the case of congressional reform by the expectation that the most powerful legislators will be most opposed to change. The more radical reforms strike directly at the prerogatives of the elective and seniority leadership of Congress. Support for such reforms is not especially widespread and comes mainly from those legislators who wield the least influence and who are also most exposed to potential sanctions from the existing leadership. Thus, the reforms of the seniority system included in our survey were all opposed by a substantial majority of the respondents. Moreover, some measures enjoyed the support of a majority of members but impinged on the leadership's prerogatives (minority-party staffing for committees was an example) and thus met with intense and powerful opposition.

The low priority given most reform measures is compounded by their low electoral payoff. The rare occasion of public excitement over congressional organization and procedures arises when a reform issue is directly linked in the public mind with a highly publicized policy conflict.

The reformist attitudes of the public reflect the paradoxical features of the internal politics of reform: as an issue, congressional reform seems most salient in times of political stalemate; yet it is precisely at such times that broad reforms are most difficult to effect, because attitudes are intense, large legislative majorities are simply not available, and energies are consumed in more immediate political conflicts. To advocate congressional change in more normal times is to tilt with windmills as far as the general public is concerned. The individual Congressman is hardly to be condemned when he concludes that his efforts on behalf of the institution and its future will go largely unobserved by his constituents.

Furthermore, Congressmen are sensitive to the latent benefits of many practices that seem nonsensical to outside observers applying abstract standards of efficiency or rationality. This sensitivity accounts for the congressional sentiment against such a "rational" measure as electronic voting or limitation on members' control of the *Congressional Record*. It may also account for some of the intense opposition to the suggestion for broadcasting and televising committee hearings. And in the same way, much of the sentiment supporting the seniority system stems from widespread recognition of the important function served by any technique that lessens conflict within Congress.

The inability to estimate accurately the effects of proposed changes also contributes to the congressional disposition not to tamper with established procedures. The Congressman, like Hamlet, is not eager to escape present ills merely to find that he has produced new and unforeseen disorders.

For these reasons, change does not typically come about through an orderly marching from basic goals through widely acknowledged problems toward agreed solutions. The fallacy of the engineering approach to reorganization is that, although its procedures can be described, they cannot always be utilized. The approach assumes a high potential for consensus on what are now widely disputed goals; it calls for comprehensive means-ends analysis involving information and foresight beyond the grasp of even the highly talented; and it presumes that members and their staffs are now, or can be, motivated to readjust radically their busy schedules and to devote near full time to a self-conscious evaluation of what to most of them is a marginal problem at best.

Yet, in spite of all the detriments to change, reform can and does occur in a variety of ways. The most frequent changes are effected through cautious tinkering with minor cogs in the legislative machinery. Modest increases in staff and office allowances, the evolution of informal party strategy committees, *ad hoc* coordination of committee work within and between the two houses—all result from an agreement on the substance of the reforms themselves as well as from a widespread consensus on the need for more "efficiency" (but *not* on the ends that are to be more efficiently served). And, as we will note later, some of the most fundamental changes of Congress have occurred gradually and almost without the awareness of the participants themselves.

Coalitions specifically for reform have been created to achieve specific modifications of rules or procedures—but only occasionally. One recent example was the 1961 enlargement (or "packing") of the House Committee on Rules to make it more responsive to the elective Democratic Party leadership in the House and to the Kennedy administration's "New Frontier" legislative program. As reported by close observers of the struggle, the narrow victory for the pro-Administration forces came only after intense struggles within the House, numerous promises and threats, and invocation of the prestige of the new President and Speaker Rayburn. Clearly, this considerable effort cannot be repeated often, in light of the multiplicity of interests and goals that converge on specific reform proposals.

Yet another mode of change can be exemplified in the events of the 89th Congress. If election results substantially alter the composition of Congress, certain reforms that in effect ratify the position of the new majority may be encouraged. New members are a strong potential source of reformist support. If these members are also liberal, or at least favorable to an activist role for government, this basic tendency to support change is intensified. The 89th Congress, which produced an increase of 38 Democratic seats in the House, clearly is a case in point. A similar, though less spectacular, turnover occurred in 1958; but at that time the new liberal members did not have the support of an activist President of their own party, nor did they possess the organizational vehicle of the Democratic Study Group to focus and coordinate their potential numerical strength. Freshman legislators, working by themselves, are unable to give direction to their aspirations; but a sizable and cohesive group of experienced members, who are prepared to make use of the additional freshman votes, can provide the necessary knowledge and experience for successful reformist activities.

A substantial change in membership is important beyond the actual number of members involved in the change. The introduction of new personnel helps to create an altered climate—a new perspective on the possibility of altering the existing institution. The attitudes of newly elected legislators and the development of optimism among the potential allies assist in encouraging potential supporters to press for changes in the rules. Much that is relevant to an understanding of the dynamics of congressional innovation can be discovered in the uniqueness of the 89th Congress.

5 THE 89TH CONGRESS AND REFORM

The materials reported in the preceding chapters were drawn largely from the 88th Congress, whose manic-depressive cycle was as foreboding as it was instructive. We have already spoken of the legislative stalemate during 1963 when editorialists were deploring the "torpid spring on Capitol Hill" and Walter Lippmann was wondering "what kind of a legislative body is it that will not or cannot legislate." The situation had changed little by November 22, when the New Frontier was deprived of its articulate young leader. Opinion surveys taken before and after President Kennedy's assassination showed mounting public dissatisfaction with congressional performance.

Yet by the time the 88th Congress collapsed in fatigue on October 3, 1964, many of its former critics were speaking of its "distinguished record of achievement." President Johnson staged a "Salute to Congress" on the White House lawn and brought out the Marine Band to play a hymn to the legislators ("Senators and Congressmen of the good old Eighty-eight/ are workin' for America, for every town and state"). The aftermath of the assassination and the succession of a "consensus" President skilled in the ways of Capitol Hill had unblocked significant legislation in civil rights, tax reduction, education, nuclear controls, urban transportation, and long-term unemployment.

The atmosphere further changed when the November

123

1964 elections produced even greater Democratic majorities in both
the House and the Senate. Of the 435 members of the House in the
88th Congress, 90 (or 21 percent) did not return for the 89th Congress because of retirement or electoral defeat. In many cases,
moderate or liberal Democrats replaced moderate or conservative
Republicans. The enlarged Democratic majority in the House at

TABLE 5.1

Support for Reform in the House,
88th and 89th Congresses*

Proportion of reform items supported	88TH CONGRESS		89TH CONGRESS (PROJECTED)	
	% of members	Number of members	% of members	Number of members
0–39% (Low)	37%	32	36%	31
40–59% (Moderate)	37	32	30	26
60–100% (High)	26	22	34	29
TOTALS	100%	86	100%	86

* The reform-support scores for the 89th Congress were computed in the following manner: 18 respondents in our original sample of the 88th Congress (21 percent) retired or were defeated in 1964—the same proportion as the actual turnover
of membership. We assigned to the freshman members of the 89th Congress (who
replaced our original respondents) support scores equivalent to the scores of
respondents with similar party and geographic characteristics. This projection
of support scores was accomplished by dividing both the low-seniority members
(1 to 5 terms) in our original sample and the 18 new freshmen into similar party
and regional categories. Reform-support scores were then assigned to the freshmen within each category in the same proportion as the distribution of support
scores of low-seniority members in the original sample. These 18 projected support
scores were then added to those of the 68 returning Congressmen in the sample,
whose support scores were presumed to have remained constant between the 88th
and 89th Congresses.

least temporarily stymied the Republican–conservative-Democrat coalition, which had frustrated a number of liberal measures throughout the 1950s and the early 1960s.

The change in the composition of the House also had a significant
impact upon the level of support for reform. Table 5.1 contrasts our
findings on the level of support in the 88th Congress for the general

notion of reform with an estimate of the extent of reformism in the
89th Congress. Our projection indicates a substantial enlargement
of the ranks of ''reformist'' members (that is, those supporting 60
to 100 percent of our 32 proposals). Thus, the internal climate for
reform in the House had changed, largely because of the substitu-
tion of strongly pro-reform Democrats for Republicans only moderately supportive of reform. The newly swollen ranks of Democratic,
liberal reformers pushed through several significant changes in
House rules and procedures. Although the Senate witnessed no
comparable changes in formal operations, the growing (and now
more senior) group of liberals moved with such authority that
many observers concluded that the old and essentially conservative
''Senate establishment'' was dead.

The 89th Congress therefore provides a convenient testing
ground for our findings on congressional reform. In 1965, no less
than four of the proposals included in our questionnaire were put
into force, in one form or another. We shall examine those aspects
of procedural change that conform to our hypotheses on the politics
of reform, as well as those aspects that seem unique to the situation
in 1965.

The House Revises Its Rules

On January 5, 1965, just minutes after the members of the House
of Representatives had received the oath of office, Majority Leader
Carl Albert of Oklahoma presented House Resolution 8, which
provided for the adoption of the rules and procedures of the
preceding Congress with three amendments. These changes were
(1) a so-called ''21-day rule'' to foreclose delays by the Committee
on Rules; (2) a method permitting bills to be sent to House-Senate
conferences without action by the Rules Committee; and (3) a
prohibition against the dilatory tactic of demanding an engrossed
copy of a bill (that is, a bill printed in its final form) before
passage. After a brief floor debate, Speaker John W. McCormack of
Massachusetts stepped down from the dais and addressed his
colleagues. In his unmistakable South Boston accents, McCormack
voiced support for the rules changes. A few moments later H. Res. 8
was agreed to by a 224–201 roll-call vote. By this simple act the
House exercised its prerogative under the constitutional guarantee

that "each House may determine the rules of its proceedings."[1]

Many outside critics viewed H. Res. 8 as hardly more than a minor palliative for what they considered Congress' fundamental ills. For those Congressmen who were veterans of the trench warfare against the inherent conservatism of the institution, however, H. Res. 8 was a long-awaited reward for years of frustration. The victory, once realized, was almost too simple; but those who had planned for it believed it to be a major step in the reconstruction of Congress. What the "new" Congress would look like, no one could predict with certainty; but the irritations that led to H. Res. 8 were familiar to all observers.

LEAN YEARS FOR THE LIBERALS

The reforms adopted by the 89th Congress can be understood only in light of the liberal discontent of the 1950s and early 1960s. All institutions are conservative, but Congress seems more impervious to change than most; and the sweeping demographic changes that altered the face of post-World War II America were reflected only imperfectly in the structure of Congress.

For one thing, most committee chairmanships have for many years been controlled by conservative elders whose one-party districts assured them of long tenure.[2] Though chairmen range from the ineffectual to the dictatorial, considerable formal powers accompany seniority positions. Most committee chairmen assume responsibility for assigning bills to subcommittees, selecting subcommittee chairmen, scheduling consideration of bills, supervising preparation of reports on bills, and finally transmitting reports to the Rules Committee. As one observer concluded:

> The House has always given great power to its committee chairmen . . . [They] have been able to help or hurt the individual Representative's chances of reelection by endorsing or repudiating specific bills. They have been able also, more importantly, to influence and even determine the nature of American law; for they have held the decisive role in the vast screening process through which all legislation has had to pass in the House.[3]

[1] Article I, Section 5.

[2] On this subject, see George Goodwin, "The Seniority System in Congress," *American Political Science Review*, 53 (June 1959), 412–436.

[3] Neil MacNeil, *Forge of Democracy* (New York: David McKay, 1963), pp. 171, 174.

There are enough detours in the legislative process so that the chairman of a substantive committee may tie up legislation for extended periods of time, and seniority leaders are not eager to yield this prerogative.

The House Rules Committee is another irritant. Dominated since the late 1930s by a conservative coalition, this committee sits at the gateway between the substantive committees and the House floor— since important bills reported by a substantive committee must be granted a "rule" that specifies the terms of the floor debate. Under the skillful direction of Judge Howard W. Smith (D-Va.), the committee consisted of an 8–4 Democratic majority during Democratic Congresses from 1955 to 1961. But this majority was deceptive since two of the Democrats—Smith and second-ranking William M. Colmer of Mississippi—often sided with the four conservative Republicans to create a deadlock on liberal measures.

Procedural devices to release measures from the Rules Committee are extremely hazardous—they have little chance of success, and they may invoke "retributions"—and thus, they have rarely been employed. A "21-day rule" adopted by the Democratic 81st Congress in 1949 permitted the chairman of a legislative committee that had reported a bill favorably to call the bill up for floor debate if the Rules Committee failed to grant a rule within 21 days. The 1950 elections depleted the liberal ranks just enough that the rule was deleted when the 82nd Congress adopted its rules in January 1951. During the two years it was in effect, the rule was invoked on eight different occasions; but the mere existence of the rule no doubt induced the Rules Committee to release other measures which it might otherwise have delayed. House liberals considered the revocation of the rule a severe setback.[4]

A third source of frustration for liberal Congressmen arose when the Senate—already more sensitive to urban interests than the House[5]—was invaded by an influx of young liberals in the late 1950s and early 1960s. This new generation of Senators encountered its own problems with the "Senate establishment," as will be

[4] For analyses of the earlier 21-day rule, see James A. Robinson, *The House Rules Committee* (Indianapolis: Bobbs-Merrill, 1963), pp. 63–71; and George B. Galloway, *The Legislative Process in Congress* (New York: Thomas Y. Crowell, 1953), pp. 343–345.

[5] See Lewis A. Froman, *Congressmen and Their Constituencies* (Chicago: Rand-McNally, 1963), pp. 69–84; and H. Douglas Price, "The Electoral Arena," in *The Congress and America's Future*, ed. David B. Truman (Englewood Cliffs, N.J.: Prentice-Hall, 1965), pp. 42–45.

seen presently. The increasingly liberal complexion of the Senate also created problems of interhouse comity as agreement by House-Senate conferees on different versions of bills passed by the two houses became more difficult to achieve. When compromises were reached, the House had its way more often than not; liberals in both bodies had frequently to decide whether a diluted bill was better than no bill at all. And in the House, motions for interhouse conferences had to revert to the Rules Committee for scheduling in the absence of unanimous consent. This scheduling power gave the Rules Committee added dilatory strength, especially during the crowded closing weeks of each session.

The 1960 election and its aftermath focused the attentions of House liberal reformers on the problem of party responsibility. Four Mississippi Democrats—William Colmer, John Bell Williams, Arthur Winstead, and Jamie Whitten—supported an unpledged slate of Presidential electors in that state. And Louisiana's famed foe of foreign aid, Representative Otto Passman, refused to back the Presidential candidate, although he refrained from announcing support for Republican nominee Richard Nixon. The Southerners' refusal to endorse the Democratic nominee was particularly irksome to liberal supporters of John Kennedy, for there was no particular local pressure on the five to back Nixon (who was hardly more acceptable than Kennedy to most voters in the Deep South).

Kennedy's narrow victory was accompanied by a loss of 20 Democratic seats in the House. When House liberals sat down shortly afterwards with Speaker Sam Rayburn to discuss ways of dealing with the Rules Committee, they suggested that the party caucus punish the five "turncoats" by stripping them of seniority and choice committee seats. This punishment would have the desired effect of ousting Colmer from the Rules Committee; and if he were replaced by a moderate, the committee deadlock could be broken. But Rayburn was firm in arguing that this alternative should be avoided because of its *ex post facto* character. The liberals relented, and the less drastic course of expanding the Rules Committee was taken. Although a floor fight was involved, this move was chosen because, as Rayburn said, it was the most "painless" procedure. The Speaker added that expansion "is a way to embarrass no one unless they want to be embarrassed."[6]

---

[6] *Congressional Quarterly Almanac, 1961,* p. 404. Accounts of the 1961 Rules Committee expansion are found in MacNeil, *Forge of Democracy,* Chapter 15; and Milton C. Cummings and Robert L. Peabody, ''The Decision to Enlarge

After a personal appeal by Rayburn on the House floor, expansion was approved by a 217–212 margin. The resulting 8–7 split was exceedingly tenuous, for the defection of a single "liberal" could reinstate the stalemate.[7] But the liberals who had urged caucus discipline of the party defectors had learned from Rayburn's teaching, and they bided their time.

THE DEMOCRATIC STUDY GROUP

A series of small, informal meetings in the fall of 1956 laid the groundwork for an organization which by 1965 was perhaps the most influential group in the House of Representatives. This organization was to become the "Democratic Study Group" (DSG), which was largely responsible for the rules changes of the 89th Congress. In many respects, the DSG's growth is linked with the course of liberal reformism in the House.

In December 1956, shortly before the 85th Congress convened, Representative Eugene J. McCarthy (Minn.) circulated among a group of his friends a statement of aims, which became known as the "Liberal Manifesto." By January 8, 1957, the document had 28 signers; and when Representative Frank Thompson, Jr. (N.J.) inserted the program in the *Congressional Record* three weeks later, the list of signers had grown to 80.[8] These liberal Democrats, many from urban areas, seemed to welcome the opportunity of articulating their own ideas on the sort of measures they thought Congress should be considering. A rudimentary and informal whip system was soon installed to implement these goals, and on June 1 the group ("McCarthy's Mavericks," as they were soon called) acquired a staff assistant. In 1958, with McCarthy deeply involved in his senatorial campaign, Representatives Thompson and Lee Metcalf (Mont.) assumed the reins of leadership. Bolstered by an influx of young liberals known as the "Class of '58," Representatives Chet Holifield (Calif.) and John A. Blatnik (Minn.) met with Speaker Rayburn early in 1959 to urge that action be taken against

---

the Committee on Rules," in *New Perspectives on the House of Representatives*, eds. Robert L. Peabody and Nelson Polsby (Chicago: Rand-McNally, 1963), pp. 167–194.

[7] The opposition on religious grounds of Representative James J. Delaney (D-N.Y.) to education-aid bills provided a good example of the instability of the committee's "liberal" majority during the 88th Congress.

[8] *Congressional Record*, 85th Congress, 1st session, 103 (January 30, 1957), 1324–1326.

the Rules Committee. Rayburn agreed to do what he could; but nothing came of the effort, partly because the overthrow of Republican Minority Leader Joseph W. Martin, Jr. (Mass.) by "gut-fighter" Charles A. Halleck (Ind.) ended the long-standing comity between Rayburn and the GOP leadership. The first session of the 86th Congress therefore saw no lessening of the liberals' frustrations.

Toward the close of the session, the liberal organization began to take shape. William Phillips, an aide to Representative George M. Rhodes (Pa.), was loaned part time and then hired full time (in May 1960) as staff director—a post he held until the end of 1965. On September 12, 1959, the Democratic Study Group was formally launched with Representative Metcalf as chairman. The following year Metcalf followed in McCarthy's footsteps and was nominated for the Senate, and Holifield succeeded him as chairman. The formal House Democratic leaders were at first suspicious that the new group might turn into an unfriendly rival. Nevertheless, as Kenneth Kofmehl remarked, "the attitudes of the House leadership toward the group . . . might best be described . . . as benevolent neutrality that grew into tacit approval."[9]

Thus matters stood until the 1960 election when the negotiations with Rayburn over punishment of the "turncoat" Southerners took place. Although they yielded to the Speaker on the tactics for dealing with the House Rules Committee, DSG leaders still hoped that expansion of the committee might lead to other rules changes that they desired. A prerequisite was the acquisition of new recruits for the liberal forces. The 1960 election resulted in a loss of 20 Democratic seats, with especially high casualties among the liberal "Class of '58." During the 1962 campaign, therefore, the DSG supplied campaign materials and other assistance to liberal Democratic candidates. Though the party lost four more House seats that year, more than 100 members were affiliated with the DSG by the beginning of the 88th Congress (a formal membership list has never been published).

Blatnik was elected DSG chairman in the spring of 1963. He and other DSG leaders were sensitive to the criticisms of legislative inaction; thus, even when the logjam broke following Kennedy's death, the liberals remained convinced that changes were needed in

[9] Kenneth Kofmehl, "The Institutionalization of a Voting Bloc," *Western Political Quarterly*, 17 (June 1964), 272. Much of the preceding summary of DSG's early history is drawn from Kofmehl's study.

congressional procedures. After all, they reasoned, a change in mood or the shift of a few seats might reinstate the old deadlock on Capitol Hill. Yet the liberals still lacked the necessary votes to control the House Democratic caucus and the 1964 elections were the key. The windfall that followed—for which Barry Goldwater was as responsible as anyone—placed the DSG at the center of reform efforts.

THE DSG MAJORITY GOES TO WORK

The same day that Lyndon Johnson received his unprecedented victory from the American electorate, a dramatic (and not unrelated) change took place in the Democratic congressional party. The Democratic majority in the House grew to 295—a gain of 38 seats; the Senate majority was increased by two, to 68. Liberal Democrats now had an undeniable majority in their party caucuses and enough votes on the floor to neutralize the old Republican–conservative-Democrat coalition.

The DSG's campaign committee, headed by Representative Richard Bolling (Mo.), had made funds of more than $70,000 available to 105 House candidates. Of the 39 incumbents receiving DSG aid, all but one were reelected; and more significantly, of the 66 nonincumbents who were helped, 40 were sent by the voters to Washington. The DSG effort involved more than financial support. Many types of campaign materials were provided, including sets of information cards on issues; "Lip from the Hip," an 80-page document containing full texts of Republican campaign arguments and suggested rebuttals; and a booklet entitled "Goldwater, Either/Or," described as a "careful compilation and analysis of the Republican candidate's controversial and contradictory statements in 16 major public-policy areas."[10] In giving aid, the DSG worked closely with the Democratic National Committee, the Democratic Senatorial and Congressional Campaign Committees, and the National Committee for an Effective Congress (a private group that supports liberal candidates of both parties). After election day, the DSG followed through by organizing a three-day orientation seminar early in the session and by giving advice to freshmen Congressmen on committee assignments, recruitment of

[10] "Activity Report—DSG Campaign Committee" (November 1964, mimeographed). See, also, National Committee for an Effective Congress, *Congressional Report*, 14 (December 2, 1965).

staff, setting up office procedures, handling constituent mail, and distribution of newsletters.

While the campaign was getting under way, an important step was taken on Capitol Hill. DSG leaders decided to arrange a caucus on party loyalty just before the members adjourned for the campaign, but the swift pace of end-of-the-session business scuttled this plan. However, on Bolling's initiative a statement was drawn up expressing the DSG's intent to purge disloyal Democratic Congressmen at the January caucus; and the day before adjournment (October 2) the statement, which had previously been mailed to all Democratic House candidates, was inserted in the *Congressional Record* by DSG Chairman Blatnik. Signed by 10 liberal Democrats, all members of DSG's Executive Committee, the declaration read in part:

> All of us are aware that, in past campaigns, some members of the Democratic caucus have openly supported presidential candidates of other political parties or independent electors in their states. This they have every right to do. We do not feel, however, that such members should be welcomed back into the Democratic fold and be entitled to committee assignments on an equal basis with those members who supported our national candidates and platform . . .
>
> We are, therefore, taking this means to serve notice of our firm intention to oppose the seating, in the January 1965 Democratic caucus, of any present member or candidate elected to the House . . . on the Democratic ticket who supported, campaigned for, or otherwise advocated the election of a President or Vice President other than the candidates nominated by the Democratic Party . . . Similar action will be directed toward any member or candidate who supported so-called unpledged or independent slates of electors . . .[11]

This statement was intended to counter the late Speaker Rayburn's argument four years earlier that a purge would be inadvisable without prior warning. The liberals hoped to neutralize pressures upon possible defectors and to set up a precedent for caucus discipline of those who did defect. "We really thought we'd catch quite a bagful," remarked one DSG member, noting the strong pressures on Southern Democrats to support Goldwater.

But beyond the immediate desire to reprimand the "turncoats"

---

[11] *Congressional Record*, 88th Congress, 2nd session (October 2, 1964, daily edition), p. 22926.

lay a long-range purpose—that of creating a new sense of party loyalty among congressional Democrats. "It was a wise, new, fresh precedent," one liberal commented. "We wanted to make the Democratic Party count for more."

The DSG's challenge was soon taken up. Three days later, Albert W. Watson, a freshman Democrat from South Carolina, announced support of Goldwater in a locally televised speech. Then Democratic Representative John Bell Williams of Mississippi made a similar statement amid considerable fanfare. As a freshman Congressman, Watson had little to lose in the way of seniority; but Williams was an 18-year veteran who, as ranking Democrat on the Commerce Committee, was next in line for the chairmanship. The thought of Williams as a possible committee chairman was hardly appealing to liberals.

The complicating factor was the possibility of Presidential intervention. After his landslide victory, President Johnson's thoughts naturally turned to reconciliation in order to gain future Southern support.[12] DSG leaders realized that White House intercession on behalf of the defectors would destroy all hopes for a purge. Publicly, Thompson expressed the hopeful prediction that the President would remain neutral: "I doubt that he would interject himself into this matter," he said. "Those of us who signed [the pre-election notice] are determined to implement it."[13] Rumors persisted, but there were no communications either to or from the White House.

The outcome of the election renewed interest in all types of reform. The votes had hardly been counted when Representative Henry Reuss (Wis.), chairman of the Democratic Platform Committee at the Atlantic City convention, recalled the party's plank on congressional reform. It read: "Congress . . . should revise its rules and procedures to assure majority rule after reasonable debate and to guarantee that major legislative proposals of the President can be brought to a vote after reasonable consideration in committee."[14] A draft list of reform proposals had been circulated among DSG members as early as September, but the end of the

[12] See Rowland Evans and Robert Novak, "To Purge or Not," *Washington Post* (November 23, 1964), p. A 13.

[13] *Washington Post* (December 4, 1964), p. A 10.

[14] U.S. Senate Library, *Factual Campaign Information* (Washington: Government Printing Office, 1964), p. 73. Reuss' remarks were reported in *Washington Post* (November 8, 1964), p. A 2.

session and the campaign had suspended discussion. On December 3, however, the DSG Executive Committee[15] held an important meeting in Chairman Blatnik's office. The agenda prepared by staff-director Phillips consisted of about 20 topics, including suggested caucus actions and House rules changes. Reuss appeared at the meeting with his own agenda, which covered much of the same ground, although it also included changes in the seniority system and provision for a special 100-vote discharge petition for measures designated by the President as essential to his program.

The two-hour meeting produced unanimous agreement on eight proposals. The following day DSG Secretary Thompson sent to all DSG members and Democratic Congressmen-elect a letter describing the package. Exclusive of the Williams-Watson purge (not mentioned in the letter), the proposals were as follows:

1. Reinstatement of the pre-1951 procedure of having the full caucus meet a second time to approve, amend, or reject the committee assignment recommendations of the Democratic Committee on Committees (which consists of the Democratic members of the Ways and Means Committee).

2. Adjustment of party ratios on House committees to reflect the more than two-to-one Democratic margin—including 17 Democrats on the 25-man Ways and Means Committee, and 34 of 50 on Appropriations.

3. Establishment of a Democratic Policy (or Steering) Committee, similar to that of the Republicans.

4. Enactment of a modified 21-day rule to unbottle the Rules Committee. Unlike the old rule, the proposal would give discretionary power to the Speaker to recognize, for the purpose of invoking the rule, any member of the committee originating the bill at issue.

5. Creation of a Joint Committee on the Organization of the Congress, modeled after the 1945 LaFollette-Monroney Committee.

6. Adoption of a rule permitting committee chairmen to offer privileged motions that, with a majority vote, would send a bill passed by both houses to a House-Senate conference.

7. Liberalization of the discharge petition to require only 175 signatures for "major measures which are a part of the majority party's legislative program," with the standard 218 signatures retained for other bills.

[15] Committee members in attendance were Bolling, William S. Moorhead (Pa.), James G. O'Hara (Mich.), Reuss, Thompson, and Morris K. Udall (Ariz.).

Although some of these changes would require approval by the full House, the crucial target was the opening Democratic caucus scheduled for the afternoon of January 2. A meeting of the entire DSG was therefore called for the morning before the Democratic caucus.

DSG strategists knew that the elected party leadership, and especially Speaker McCormack, must be kept informed. "There's no use trying to do things behind the Speaker's back," one observer commented. "He'll find out anyway." Thus, the first formal approach to the leadership came on December 15 when two DSG Executive Committee members had lunch with Majority Whip Hale Boggs of Louisiana, who is close to the Speaker. The liberals hoped to soften his expected objections to parts of the reform package and were somewhat surprised, therefore, when toward the close of their discussion they realized that the Southerner had indicated support for seven of the eight proposals and had expressed apprehension only about changing the party ratio on Ways and Means. Boggs reasoned that the votes to pass Medicare were already assured and that if necessary a discharge petition could blast the bill out of the Ways and Means Committee. More important, he felt that being "hard-nosed" about committee ratios might set an unfortunate precedent: if the Democrats were again in the minority, the Republicans might well reciprocate with a vengeance. What most struck the liberals was Boggs' acceptance of the Williams-Watson purge and his readiness to allow caucus approval of committee assignments. As for the purge, he explained that many of his fellow Southerners who had "stuck their necks out" to support President Johnson would be more than happy to see the defectors punished. A secret ballot in the caucus, he felt, would enhance the chances for success.

The DSG members were also counseled by the Whip on tactics. First, the DSG should designate a "safe" Congressman like Blatnik as their leader in the caucus, keeping the "ultra-liberal" types in the background. Second, Representative Eugene J. Keogh of New York, McCormack's choice as chairman of the caucus, should be checked out to soften his resistance to the reforms. (Many liberals believed that Keogh had a tacit standing agreement with the Southerners and that he might oppose the purge in order to protect the seniority system. But whatever the reason, Keogh's opposition never materialized.) Finally, the Speaker should be consulted and assured that the proposed changes would strengthen his own position and that the DSG had the needed caucus votes.

Holifield and Blatnik, who had served before as go-betweens and had earned the Speaker's confidence, were dispatched to negotiate with McCormack. They met on three successive days between Christmas and New Year's to discuss the proposals. Before each session, several DSG activists gathered in Blatnik's office to review the lines of argument. After the two negotiators departed for the Speaker's Chambers, the others waited tensely; when they returned, the results were mulled over carefully. For the second and third meetings, McCormack brought in House Parliamentarian Lewis Deschler to refine the DSG's preliminary drafts of the rules changes. "When Deschler showed up, we knew we were making progress," one DSG man said.

McCormack favored reinstatement of the 21-day rule—he had announced support for it publicly following the election. At first he balked at the discretionary feature of the new rule, but he yielded to Blatnik's and Holifield's vigorous arguments for strengthening the Speaker's powers. He also endorsed the change in conference report procedure and a provision that would "deprive any member of the privilege of demanding a fully engrossed copy of a bill." Not a part of the liberals' package, this latter proposal was added at the insistence of Representative Neal Smith (D-Iowa), who lobbied personally with the Speaker to obtain it. Smith wanted to prevent the dilatory tactic—employed most notably by Representative H. R. Gross (R-Iowa)—of asking for an engrossed copy of a bill in order to hold up final passage for 24 hours.

The Speaker pledged neutrality in the Williams-Watson affair, but he advised that stripping the two of seniority on their committees would be sufficient punishment. He argued that refusing caucus seating would be more controversial and would only serve to make martyrs of the two men. DSG leaders were coming to the same conclusion. As one of them reasoned, "We bought neutrality from the leadership by agreeing to go for seniority rather than caucus seating. We weren't really after those two . . ."

Many DSG leaders viewed the opportunity of reviewing committee assignments as the most important item in the reform package. Two objectives were involved in this seemingly innocent proposal: first, it would assure that the Committee on Committees followed caucus instructions on the Williams-Watson assignments; and second, it would reestablish a precedent for future party control of committee assignments. McCormack agreed to work out new committee ratios with the Republican leadership, and he promised to call a second Democratic caucus to ratify the report of the Committee on Committees. According to his interpretation, the caucus rules already provided for review of committee assignments, although the practice had been unused since 1951. He therefore asked that no motion be offered for a second caucus.

McCormack was cool toward the steering-committee proposal if the group was to be given decision-making powers (he had opposed the proposal two years earlier). He was also reluctant to endorse the discharge-petition idea since it would give him added discretion in naming those issues considered "major measures" eligible for a reduced number of signatures. The DSG representatives raised informally the possibility of applying a liberalized discharge petition solely to the District of Columbia Committee since District home rule was the only important liberal measure that was not expected to get out of committee. Deschler contended, however, that no rule should be drawn to apply to a single committee.

The meetings with McCormack laid the groundwork for a liberal victory in the caucus and on the House floor. No explicit "treaties" had been signed, but the bargains had nonetheless been struck in the subtle, roundabout manner so familiar to Congressmen. The Speaker and the DSG knew each other's strengths and worked to preserve comity. On New Year's Day, the DSG sponsored a reception at the National Capitol Democratic Club in honor of the newly elected Democratic Congressmen and their wives. To everyone's surprise, McCormack was one of the first to arrive, and he stationed himself at the door to greet the newcomers. His presence was symbolic, and an air of confident anticipation prevailed.

THE CHANGES ARE ADOPTED

At 10 A.M. on January 2, the newly enlarged DSG gathered for the first time in Room 1302 of the Longworth House Office Building —the very room where the DSG had held its first organizing session in 1959. So many members poured in that a number were forced to stand throughout the 1½-hour session. More than 150 were present —enough to control that afternoon's Democratic caucus.

DSG Chairman Blatnik opened the meeting and yielded to Thompson, who proceeded to introduce the DSG's senior members. Then the senior Representative from each state introduced his freshman delegation. The formalities concluded, Blatnik reviewed the reform proposals and outlined the available stratagems.

One by one the proposals were agreed to. The matter of party ratios on the committees was not pressed because the Speaker had assured the DSG leaders that he would take care of it through negotiations with GOP leaders. Also deleted was the request for a second party caucus to review committee assignments: the Speaker had promised to call the caucus himself.

The proposal to reduce to 175 the number of signatures needed for certain discharge petitions was then debated. Some members thought a liberalized rule would allow many undesirable measures to reach the House floor.[16] Others quibbled over the number of signatures—some favored 190, others 175. A show of hands was requested, and opinions were so divided that the proposal was dropped from the package. Actually, liberal strategists assumed that the 218 signatures necessary under the current rule could be obtained to free the District home-rule bill—the main target of the proposal for discharge-petition reform. (This assumption proved correct when a home rule bill was discharged later in the session, but a further assumption—that home rule could be passed once it reached the floor—proved erroneous.) DSG leaders conceded afterwards that dropping the discharge proposal was a wise tactical move. ''As it turned out,'' one said, ''the package had all it could carry. Pressing for the discharge change might well have cost us the whole package.''

On the other proposals there was unanimous approval. If accepted by the caucus, the rules changes would be presented as a resolution at the opening session of the entire House. The Williams-Watson purge would also be pressed at the caucus. No immediate action was required on two of the items: the Joint Committee on the Organization of the Congress would be created through normal legislative action (S. Con. Res. 2), and the Democratic Steering Committee idea would have to be explored informally.

The Democratic caucus met in the House chamber at 2:30 that afternoon. The first crucial vote was whether to ballot secretly on the disciplining of Williams and Watson, since members might hesitate to vote against the two if their votes were known. The

---

[16] The committees are counted upon to pigeonhole most bills introduced. Some measures would be difficult to oppose on the floor—increased veterans' pensions and the school-prayer amendment are two examples—and many Congressmen prefer not to have to take a public stand on them.

secret ballot won handily, and when the vote was taken it was
157–115 in favor of stripping Williams and Watson of their
seniority. The *New York Times* called the move "an important first
step toward establishing party responsibility in the 89th Congress."[17] Representative Harley O. Staggers of West Virginia
would replace Williams as second-ranking Democrat on the Commerce Committee. When it was learned the following summer that
Commerce Committee Chairman Oren Harris planned to retire, one
DSG member quipped, "Oren should really be grateful to us."
Because of Williams' unpopularity, Harris would have been under
great pressure to retain his chairmanship. (Earlier there were
rumors that Harris might appoint Williams a subcommittee chairman in spite of the fact that the latter now stood at the foot of the
committee's seniority list. Harris was quietly warned that the
caucus could review this action and instruct the committee to
comply with the spirit of the purge. The appointment was never
made.)

After the caucus, Watson told reporters he would leave the party
rather than remain a "second-class Democrat." Subsequently, he
resigned his seat, ran in the special election as a Republican, and
was elected. His 2nd District of South Carolina has supported
Republican presidential candidates since 1952. Williams, whose
state of Mississippi gave the Republican presidential candidate 87
percent of the vote in 1964, decided to remain in the Democratic
ranks for the time being. By early 1966, however, he was demanding that House Democrats restore his seniority in the 90th Congress
—an action through which he would replace Staggers as Commerce
Committee chairman. "I will accept no less," Williams declared on
the House floor. "I have no intention of climbing that ladder again,
rung by rung."[18] Behind the actions of Watson and Williams lay
the increasing Republican pressures being felt in a number of
Southern districts. But so long as the Democratic margin in the
House remained large, it was unlikely that the liberals in control of
the caucus would be moved by such threats.

No move was made to waive the second Democratic caucus. The
Speaker's bargain was made good. Apparently the more conserva-
tive and seniority-minded members had decided not to oppose the
Speaker. Or perhaps they simply weren't aware of the implications

of the move. "This was the sleeper in the whole package," said one DSG aide of the review caucus. "It was pretty much overlooked by everyone." Whatever the explanation, the DSG had won recognition of the right of the caucus to ratify committee assignments. By objecting to one of the assignments, perhaps a chairmanship, an attack could be launched on the seniority system itself.

The caucus also agreed by a 189–71 vote to submit the three rules changes—the 21-day rule, the conference-report rule, and the engrossed-copy rule—to the House. The next task was to obtain favorable House action on the changes. As the *New York Times* stated editorially, "How vigorously the rules battle is pressed on Capitol Hill will help determine how well this Congress fulfills its responsibility for letting majority will rule on all measures vital to the national welfare."[19]

The opening day of the new Congress was deceptively routine. After the Clerk called the House to order and the Chaplain offered the prayer, the roll of Representatives-elect was called by states. The next order of business was the election of a Speaker from the candidates nominated by the two party caucuses. On a straight party vote, and to no one's surprise, McCormack was duly re-elected. Minority Leader Gerald R. Ford of Michigan gracefully introduced McCormack, who took the oath of office administered by the dean of the House, Emanuel Celler (D-N.Y.).

Shortly thereafter, Majority Leader Albert rose to present the resolution embodying the rules changes.[20] Then Judge Smith countered with a defense of his Rules Committee. "The 21-day rule I am opposed to," he said. "We had it once, we used it for one Congress, then it was abandoned as not workable." The late Clarence J. Brown of Ohio, ranking Republican on Rules, then argued that the change would give the Speaker inordinate powers. When McCormack stepped down from the dais to defend the change, calling the new discretionary power "a reasonable provision," Brown replied that "We gave that power to 'Uncle Joe' Cannon and Tom Reed, as the gentleman recalls. We gave them too much power." After several minutes of debate, the yeas and nays were ordered and the clerk called the roll. By a vote of 224–201, H. Res. 8 passed and the liberals had won an important victory. The *Times* proclaimed that the House "struck a blow for one of the

---

[19] *New York Times* (January 4, 1965), p. 28.

[20] The events described here are found in *Congressional Record*, 89th Congress, 1st session (January 4, 1965, daily edition), p. 19.

most important of its own civil liberties—namely, the right to vote."[21]

New party ratios for all committees were fixed at a conference of both parties' leaders the next day: Ways and Means went from 15–10 to 17–8, and Appropriations from 30–20 to 34–16. In a few weeks a new Democratic Steering Committee was created. Chaired by Representative Ray J. Madden (Ind.), the group consisted of six *ex officio* voting members (Speaker, Majority Leader, Whip, Chairman and Secretary of the Caucus, and Chairman of the Campaign Committee) and 18 regional representatives—generally the deans of the geographic areas. One DSG leader predicted that the group would collapse; but another expressed the belief that although the group was "not all it could be, it's not a fiasco either." The President held monthly meetings with the Steering Committee during 1965 to give members a full view of the legislative program. In late August the House quietly authorized a full-time staff member for the Steering Committee.[22] Only time could determine, however, whether the group could assume real authority.

On January 18, the Speaker called a special caucus to ratify committee assignments made by the Committee on Committees. DSG leaders carefully weighed the alternatives and decided not to challenge any of the recommendations. It was felt that the mere precedent of having the second caucus would be sufficient for the time being. The review caucus could conceivably be employed in the future to challenge certain assignments on a selective basis. "We'll pick a target, amend a committee list, and set still another precedent," a DSG leader predicted.

The package of rules changes adopted in 1965 was the product of various motives and pressures, though certainly urban, liberal, Inventor types were disproportionately found within the DSG. One DSG member observed that two schools of thought on congressional reform had emerged within the liberal camp: "There are the caucus reformers and the rules reformers," he said. "This time we went down both roads at once."

Some liberals, including Wisconsin's Reuss, favored formal rules

[21] *New York Times* (January 5, 1965), p. 32. On the roll call, 23 Southern Democrats and 16 Republicans voted with the majority. Of the Northern Democrats, only three opposed the changes.

[22] H. Res. 543. A staff member was also provided for the House Republican Policy Committee. See *Congressional Record*, 89th Congress, 1st session (August 24, 1965, daily edition), p. 20747.

changes as the best method for speeding up the legislative process. The 21-day rule was such a change, as were the alterations in conference-report and engrossed-copy procedures. However, others in the liberal camp—including Bolling, Morris K. Udall of Arizona, and James G. O'Hara of Michigan—leaned toward a strengthening of party responsibility through the caucus. From their point of view, the precedents established in the caucus, if retained, were a potentially more significant development than the more spectacular rules changes. The "caucus reformers" may indeed have the greater opportunity to work their will in the future; for while the Republicans can recover the strength they lost in the wake of the Johnson landslide, the chances are good that, as one member put it, "the liberals will control the Democratic caucus for as long as we can see." Viewing the events of January 1965, two well-known Washington columnists concluded that "the subject of congressional reform—along with the DSG—is being approached with new respect on Capitol Hill."[23]

GOP REFORMISM IN THE HOUSE

Lest the emphasis of this chapter be misleading, it should be pointed out that the Democrats have no monopoly on congressional reformism. Yet the 1964 elections so depleted the Republican forces —especially in the House—that in the 89th Congress the minority party encountered unusual difficulties in making itself heard. Even the threat of the Republican–conservative-Democrat coalition was muted because on most issues the Northern wing of the Democratic Party could command an absolute majority.

Obviously apprehensive about a majority stampede, the House Republican Conference announced, on December 16, 1964, a series of five minority "fair play" proposals: (1) to give the ranking minority members of committees time equal to that controlled by committee chairmen during floor debates on conference reports; (2) to continue efforts to obtain a "more generous allowance for minority staffing on legislative committees"; (3) to forbid House consideration of nongermane amendments added by the Senate to House measures; (4) to allow any member sponsoring an amendment five minutes to explain it on the floor (in order to prevent the

[23] Rowland Evans and Robert Novak, "The Liberal House," *Washington Post* (January 6, 1965), p. A 17.

shutting off of debate) ; and (5) to insist upon a full five-day work week—thus ending the "Tuesday-to-Thursday club" of members who return to their districts every weekend.[24] Spokesmen for the conference promised to introduce resolutions embodying these reforms, but nothing was heard of them after the December 16 statement.

Ideological distinctions among congressional Republicans are somewhat more subtle than the differences among Democrats; but it is fair to generalize that Republican reformism has been concentrated among a talented group of young and middle-seniority Congressmen who view the minority party's role as a vigorous one of developing and publicizing constructive policy alternatives. By and large, these members have been identified with the elevation to party leadership of Representative Gerald Ford of Michigan—a move that required deposing Charles Hoeven of Iowa as Conference (caucus) Chairman in 1963 and then Charles Halleck of Indiana as Floor Leader in 1965.[25] These "Young Turks" are drawn from all ranges of the ideological spectrum, although the moderate and liberal wings of the party are undoubtedly predominant.

Perhaps the most persistent concern of reform-minded House Republicans has been the nurturing of research and policy-making groups within their own party structure.[26] As a result of the leadership changes surrounding Ford's election as Floor Leader, there were in 1965 two Republican policy bodies in the House: the old Republican Policy Committee (chaired by Representative John J. Rhodes of Arizona), which was concerned with day-to-day policy making; and the newly created Committee on Planning and Research (headed by Representative Charles E. Goodell of New York), which undertook long-range research.

One of the Republicans most intimately identified with congressional reorganization has been Representative Thomas B. Curtis of Missouri. In 1961, he and Representative Chet Holifield (D-Calif.) launched a series of dinner meetings on the subject and invited a number of interested House members as well as representatives of the

[24] See *Congressional Quarterly Weekly Report*, 1 (January 1, 1965), 3.

[25] See Robert L. Peabody, *The Ford-Halleck Minority Leadership Contest, 1965*, Eagleton Institute Case Study No. 40 (New York: McGraw-Hill, 1966).

[26] For developments through the 88th Congress, consult Charles O. Jones, *Party and Policy-Making* (New Brunswick, N.J.: Rutgers University Press, 1964).

American Political Science Association. This group discussed long-range bipartisan approaches to reform and eventually stimulated the APSA's extensive "Study of Congress" in 1964.

A somewhat more formal group was the Republican Committee on Minority Staffing, created in 1963 as an arm of the House Republican Conference. A number of Republicans—including Curtis and Fred Schwengel (Iowa)—had urged creation of such a group; and one of Ford's first acts as Conference Chairman was to establish the committee with Schwengel as chairman. This group lobbied for increased minority staff personnel for committees and was often constrained to argue with conservative-minded, ranking Republican committee members. In April 1965, this group was reconstituted as the Task Force on Congressional Reform and Minority Staffing.[27] Working in loose cooperation with outside scholars and with the Joint Committee on the Organization of the Congress, the task force undertook research and sponsored reports by its members on various aspects of reorganization—bipartisan as well as partisan in nature.

The Senate: An Old Order Passes

Senator Joseph S. Clark relates that when he first arrived in the Senate in January 1957, he and the five other freshman Democrats were treated to a luncheon by then-Majority Leader Lyndon Johnson. As the newcomers sat down to their steaks, they found at each place a copy of *Citadel: The Story of the U.S. Senate*, a book by journalist William S. White.[28] The books were inscribed "with all good wishes" not only by the author, but also by Johnson, who urged the Senators "to consider Mr. White's book as a sort of *McGuffey's Reader* from which [they] could learn much about 'the greatest deliberative body in the world.' '' He also counseled them to "mold" themselves into the Senate's "way of life."[29] It was not

---

[27] Officially the group worked under the Republican Planning and Research Committee. During the 89th Congress its chairman was Representative James C. Cleveland (N.H.). Though the group's official membership list included eight names, no less than two-dozen Republicans (including two ex-Congressmen, Fred Schwengel of Iowa and John V. Lindsay of New York) actually participated and were, to all intents and purposes, "members."

[28] (New York: Harper & Row, 1957).

[29] Related in Clark's *Congress: The Sapless Branch* (New York: Harper & Row, 1964), p. 5.

long before Clark and his colleagues learned the meaning of Johnson's gesture.

White's volume was the culmination of what has been called his public love affair with the United States Senate. It propagated the theory that a shadowy "inner club" ran the Senate according to a set of genteel norms, which closely approximated Speaker Rayburn's maxim that the successful legislator is one who learns to "go along." The book was highly laudatory of Johnson, White's fellow Texan; and, in line with the familiar demonology of the author's syndicated column, White contended that the essentially conservative "inner club" performed the useful task of bridling the enthusiasms of the "Young Turk" liberals. Other commentators produced considerable evidence that the "inner circle's" norms of behavior were an influential aspect of senatorial life in the postwar years.[30]

Some writers have disputed the existence of White's inner club. The Senate, from White's own testimony, is exceedingly tolerant of diversity; and any rough listing of senatorial "leaders" will reveal a variety of personality types, leadership styles, and policy preferences.[31] While many young Senators have elected to serve their apprenticeships gracefully and docilely,[32] others have explicitly chosen the role of the "outsider"—preferring to exert influence *upon* the institution if not *within* it.

Clark made such a choice, as did William Proxmire of Wisconsin. Both men made explicit decisions, as the latter expressed it, to "be a Senator like Wayne [Morse] and Paul [Douglas]."[33] They were not alone, and like most "outsiders" they soon became disgruntled believers in White's thesis. Clark, for example, was hopeful that the election of a number of young liberals in 1958 would change the Senate's power structure. But largely through manipulation of committee assignments, the "club" retained its influence virtually intact. The high point in Clark's heresy came in February 1963, when he took the Senate floor to denounce the "Senate estab-

[30] See especially Donald R. Matthews, *U.S. Senators and Their World* (Chapel Hill: University of North Carolina Press, 1960), Chap. 5.

[31] Nelson Polsby, *Congress and the Presidency* (Englewood Cliffs, N.J.: Prentice-Hall, 1964), Chap. 3.

[32] Senator Edward M. Kennedy's (D-Mass.) early tactics as a freshman are reported in Ernest G. Warren, "Senator Ted Accepts 'Freshman' Role," *Boston Herald* (January 8, 1963), p. 3.

[33] Ralph K. Huitt, "The Outsider in the Senate—An Alternative Role," *American Political Science Review*, 55 (September 1961), 566–575.

lishment" in a series of widely publicized (if poorly attended) speeches.[34] There were still unbelievers when Clark finished, but there could be little question that the notion of a tight, conservative, ruling clique had become an obsession with liberals, who found themselves on the outside.

THE COMMITTEE-ASSIGNMENT CONTROVERSY

The immediate target of Clark's attack was an intricate series of maneuvers over committee assignments at the beginning of the 88th Congress. Liberal Democrats believed that the increase in Democratic seats from the 1962 elections should be reflected in a readjustment of committee party ratios. Rather than unseating low-ranking Republicans, they called for expansion of three key committees: Finance (17 to 21), Appropriations (27 to 29), and Foreign Relations (17 to 21). By appointing Democrats to the new slots, a change in party ratios could be effected without unseating any Republicans. The makeup of Finance was of special concern since this committee was to consider President Kennedy's tax-reform bill, which was high on the Administration's list of priorities.

The 15-member Senate Democratic Steering Committee, which draws up committee assignments, had a strongly conservative coloration. Five of the seven Southerners in the group were themselves committee chairmen; two nonSouthern chairmen were also members. Only six members, including Clark, could be classified as consistently liberal. Yet Clark estimated that only 27 of the 67 Democratic Senators could be classed "conservatives."[35] He charged that the Steering Committee was unrepresentative of the increasingly liberal Senate Democratic contingent. He pointed out that in 1961, and again in 1963, the Democratic Conference had approved a resolution that the Steering Committee reflect the geographic and ideological views of all Senate Democrats.

Clark further contended that Senators who had voted for a liberalized cloture rule early in 1963 were passed over for favorable committee assignments.[36] During his "establishment" speech, Clark

[34] Reprinted as *The Senate Establishment* (New York: Hill & Wang, 1963).

[35] For background information, see *Congressional Quarterly Weekly Report* (March 1, 1963), pp. 237–238.

[36] The liberals believed, and later charged publicly, that then-Secretary to the Majority Robert G. Baker actually falsified their requests for committee assignments. When the Steering Committee meets, a large chart is prepared listing all committee vacancies and the names of Senators wishing new

produced a chart showing that, of the eight nonfreshman Democrats who had voted against easing the cloture rule and had also requested new committee assignments, seven received new assignments and six were given their first choice. But of the 14 nonfreshmen who had favored easing cloture and had asked for new assignments, only five were granted their requests; and only one, Majority Leader Mike Mansfield (Mont.), received his first choice.[37] Clark neglected to mention, however, that the seven (out of nine) freshman Democrats who voted with the liberals received the major committee posts they wanted as a result of an informal policy of assuring each new Democratic Senator at least one major committee assignment—the so-called "Johnson rule," which had been initiated by Majority Leader Johnson in 1953.

On February 13, 1963, the Steering Committee rejected Mansfield's motion to enlarge the Finance Committee from 17 to 19 (adding two Democrats and retaining the six Republicans). The Majority Leader said the vote against the proposal was "very substantial" and declared that the plan had been his own and not the President's—as had been rumored.[38] One observer called the Steering Committee's action the product of a "privately arranged political double play between the conservative Republicans and the Southern Democrats . . ."[39] Reportedly, Minority Leader Everett M. Dirksen (Ill.) decided he wanted the one vacant Republican seat on Finance and so informed Mansfield and the Southerners. Enlargement of the committee would have negated Dirksen's conservative vote, and so it was agreed to leave the committee at 17 members. Ironically, the Steering Committee did agree to change the ratio on Appropriations from 17–10 to 18–9. This change had the effect of bumping from the committee Senator Jacob K. Javits (N.Y.), lowest-ranking Republican and a liberal.

When Clark condemned this power play on the Senate floor, Mansfield entered a rejoinder. "It is all very well," he said, "for Senators to immerse themselves in household management. But I

---

assignments—along with their first, second, and subsequent choices. Since Baker prepared the chart, he was in a position to omit key requests made by certain Senators. *Washington Post* (November 15, 1963), p. A 1.

[37] *Congressional Record*, 88th Congress, 1st session, 109 (February 20, 1963), 2670.

[38] *Boston Herald* (February 15, 1963), p. 1. The Steering Committee vote was reportedly 10–5. *Washington Post* (February 15, 1963), p. A 1.

[39] Rowland Evans in *Washington Post* (February 16, 1963), p. A 2.

think it is about time for someone to remind the Senate of its higher responsibilities under the Constitution."[40] The Senate finally rejected by a 68–17 vote Clark's amendment to expand the Finance Committee from 17 to 21 members (14 Democrats and seven Republicans); and by a 70–12 vote it rejected a similar bid to expand Appropriations from 27 to 29 members. Clark withdrew his amendment to reconstitute Foreign Relations—a committee assignment he himself desired.[41] Then a resolution (S. Res. 90) setting the size of all other standing committees was passed by a voice vote. The committee assignment controversy ended in a temporary defeat for the liberal forces.

BATTLE OVER CLOTURE

The Senate's biennial battle over Rule XXII, which governs limitation of debate, began on January 14, 1963, when Senator Clinton P. Anderson (D-N.M.) introduced a resolution (S. Res. 9) to lower the majority needed to invoke cloture from two thirds to three fifths of those Senators present and voting.[42] Proposals for changing Senate rules at the beginning of a session face a thorny procedural dilemma: "Do the rules of a previous Congress automatically govern proposals to change the rules at the outset of a new Congress? . . . If not, then a filibuster could be stopped by a majority vote, and the substantive proposals for changes in the rules [could be] voted on."[43] The question turns on whether the Senate is a "continuing body." Since the House has a totally "new" membership with each new Congress, it must adopt rules every two years. But because two thirds of the Senators are incumbent at the start of each Congress, it has been questioned whether the Senate must adopt new rules. The Senate has usually elected to proceed as a "continuing body"; but if it chose not to do so, "unlimited debate" would not be in effect until the rules were adopted, and debate could be cut off by the normal parliamentary method of a majority vote.

[40] *Washington Post* (February 21, 1963), p. A 2.

[41] *Washington Post* (February 26, 1963), p. A 4.

[42] The Senate, of course, prides itself on its "unlimited debate." Under the present Rule XXII, debate may be closed by an elaborate procedure. A petition must be signed by 16 Senators, and then the question of cloture is brought up two days later. Two thirds of the Senators present and voting must agree to the motion, after which each Senator still has up to one hour of remarks on the issue at hand.

[43] *Congressional Quarterly Weekly Report* (January 18, 1963), p. 73.

The liberals sought from the presiding officer, Vice President Lyndon Johnson, a ruling that a majority could shut off debate on a rules change. Johnson handed the question back to the Senate —a course usually favored by Senate presiding officers. Johnson declared:

> It is a matter for the Senators. The Vice President cannot tell Senators how to make up their minds. He cannot make rules for the Senate that the Senate has not made for itself. Nothing in the Consitution gives the Vice President the power to determine when he thinks the Senators have talked enough.[44]

After three weeks of debate, the liberals failed by 10 votes to invoke cloture and to end the conservative filibuster over the rules change.[45] According to Senator Clark, it was this vote that was used against pro-cloture Senators in committee assignments.

In the 89th Congress the liberals again pressed for amendment of Rule XXII with substantially the same results. Many thought the effort was merely an exercise in frustration:

> The renewed fight against filibustering in the Senate suffers from psychological weariness. Liberals in the Senate have walked up this hill so many times in recent decades that their struggle has come to seem ritualistic.[46]

One bizarre incident in the 1965 controversy deserves mention, however. The liberals hoped that by delaying their request for a ruling from the chair until after the Inauguration they could induce Hubert Humphrey, the new Vice President and a former colleague, to rule in favor of simple majority cloture on rules amendments.[47] On January 6, Anderson again introduced his resolution to reduce to three fifths the majority needed for cloture. Senator Dirksen objected to "immediate consideration" of Anderson's amendment. This parliamentary tactic meant that unless action could be completed during the so-called "morning hour" the

[44] Quoted in *New York Times* (January 7, 1963), p. 19.

[45] The vote was 54–42 in favor of cloture, short of the needed two-thirds majority. *Congressional Record*, 88th Congress, 1st session, 109 (February 7, 1963), 2058.

[46] Editorial, *Washington Post* (January 4, 1965), p. A 10.

[47] Needless to say, there was no assurance that Humphrey would so rule. After Johnson's ruling in 1963, Humphrey was quoted as saying that he was not certain he wanted to give the Vice President the power to close debate. "I should like the Senate itself to face the responsibility," he stated. Cited in *Washington Post* (December 31, 1964), p. A 1.

following day, the proposal would be placed on the calendar and
further delays would ensue.

As soon as routine business had been transacted the next day,
Dirksen moved to send Anderson's resolution to the Committee on
Rules and Administration. The Republican Leader announced that
his purpose was to see S. Res. 6 "buried in the deepest, deepest
grave with enough earth over it so that we will never see its ugly
face again."[48] Anderson countered with an amendment to Dirksen's
motion directing the Rules Committee to report the resolution by
January 25, after the Inauguration. The amendment further
stipulated that when the committee reported, "all rights in existence at the opening of Congress shall be deemed preserved."
Senator Richard B. Russell (D-Ga.), one of the Senate's masters of
parliamentary procedure, inquired whether this amendment was
not out of order. President Pro Tem Carl Hayden (D-Ariz.), who
was in the chair, answered inaudibly. At this moment Hayden
declared the "morning hour" closed, and Anderson's resolution
was placed on the calendar.

A few moments later Senator Douglas claimed to have heard a
rumor that Hayden had ruled Anderson's amendment out of order.
Since the transcript was not yet ready, Majority Leader Mansfield
called a brief recess. Douglas rushed to the Senate Reporters' room
and found that Hayden had indeed ruled against the Anderson
amendment. When the session resumed, Douglas asked for permission to question the reporter and journal clerk—an unheard-of
procedure. Tempers flared, and Mansfield moved for a second
recess. The dispute was finally resolved when it was agreed to send
the Anderson resolution, along with S. Res. 8 (which would lower to
a simple majority the vote needed for cloture), to the Rules
Committee. Two months later, both resolutions were reported
adversely by the committee; no further action was taken.[49]

Though the rule itself proved intractable, cloture was successfully invoked three times in the early 1960s: in 1962 an unusual
liberal filibuster over the communications satellite bill was termi-
nated under Rule XXII by a bipartisan coalition; after a two-and-
a-half-month Southern stand against the Civil Rights Act of 1964,

---

[48] Quoted in E. W. Kenworthy's excellent account, *New York Times*
(January 8, 1965).

[49] Senate Reports 74 and 75 (89th Congress, 1st session). Both reports were
accompanied by minority views from Senators Clark and Hugh Scott (R-Pa.)
and additional views of Senator John Sherman Cooper (R-Ky.).

cloture was again successfully invoked; and on May 25, 1965, a 70–30 cloture vote shut off debate on the Voting Rights Act of 1965. As long as the present cloture rule is in effect, liberals themselves have not been hesitant to resort to filibusters. As Clark explained, "Why should I tie both my hands behind my back? I'm in favor of changing the rule, but until they change it I'm going to play the game according to the rules."[50]

SOME SMALL SUCCESSES

Several marginal alterations in Senate rules have been effected in recent years. In January 1963, for example, Majority Leader Mansfield appointed an "Ad Hoc Committee for the Expeditious Handling of Senate Business." Chaired by Senator A. S. Mike Monroney (D-Okla.), the group met informally in the early weeks of the session and arrived at a number of proposals for speeding up legislative business. One of the recommendations (S. Res. 89) was to amend Senate Rule VIII so that "germane" debate would be required during a four-hour period following the morning hour. During this time Senators would restrict their remarks to the business at hand. Introduced by Senator John O. Pastore (D-R.I.) and a large bipartisan group of Senators, this resolution was approved by the Rules and Administration Committee. The committee, however, reduced to three hours the period during which germaneness would be required and exempted amendments from the requirement (so as not to prohibit legislative "riders").[51] S. Res. 89 was adopted in early 1964 by a 57–25 roll call vote.[52]

A week later the Senate passed S. Res. 111, which amended Senate Rule XXV to permit standing committees to meet during floor sessions until completion of the morning hour. Formerly, unanimous consent was needed to allow committees to meet while the Senate was in session. Such permission was typically granted, but it could be refused whenever a single Senator failed to give his consent. Sponsored by Senator Frank Church (D-Idaho), the resolution was adopted by a 47–35 vote.[53] A third recommendation of the Monroney group was enacted in late 1963. This resolution (S.

---

[50] Quoted in *Washington Post* (May 31, 1965), p. A 7.

[51] *Congressional Quarterly Weekly Report* (October 4, 1963), p. 1713.

[52] *Congressional Record*, 88th Congress, 2nd session, 110 (January 23, 1964), 1076.

[53] *Congressional Record*, 110 (January 30, 1964), 1409.

Res. 78), introduced by Senator Claiborne Pell (D-R.I.), authorized former Presidents to address the Senate after giving appropriate prior notice to the presiding officer. It was passed by a voice
vote on October 1, 1963.[54]
In the fall of 1963, disclosures of the activities of Robert G.
Baker, then Secretary to the Majority, set off a rash of journalistic
and public demands for a new look at congressional ethics. The
Senate's own inquiry into the "Bobby Baker scandal," sparked by
Senator John J. Williams (R-Del.), generated much publicity but
failed to resolve the lurking question of senatorial involvement in
Baker's dealings. (Republicans charged that Democrats on the
Rules Committee were trying to avoid implicating President
Johnson, who as Majority Leader had hired Baker.) However, the
Senate did create, in July 1964, a bipartisan "watchdog committee" to oversee the conduct of members. It was unclear what the
group's exact duties would be: a year passed before the membership
was chosen, and it was four more months before the first organizing
meeting was held.[55] Yet the very existence of the committee gave
new impetus to efforts to enact a formal "code of conduct" for
Senators. Advocates of full disclosure of personal finances, including Senators Clark and Clifford P. Case (R-N.J.), were especially
active in working for such a code.

END OF THE "ESTABLISHMENT"?

While revisions of Senate rules and procedures were not as
spectacular as those in the House, the complexion of the body has
changed markedly since the publication of White's book. Whether
the "Senate establishment" ever existed as an identifiable group is,
as we have suggested, a question not easily resolved. The perquisites
of seniority in the Senate are, of course, formidable—though
somewhat less so than in the larger House of Representatives. And
undoubtedly an individual's chances for influence in the Senate are
enhanced by "playing the game" according to the institutional
norms. Whether these realities add up to a sinister conspiracy,
which systematically deprives liberals of useful power, is question-

[54] *Congressional Quarterly Weekly Report* (October 4, 1963), p. 1742.

[55] Members of the committee are John Stennis (D-Miss.), chairman;
Wallace F. Bennett (R-Utah), vice chairman; A. S. Mike Monroney (D-
Okla.); John Sherman Cooper (R-Ky.); Eugene J. McCarthy (D-Minn.); and
James B. Pearson (R-Kan.).

able. Of this much one can be certain. At some point in the mid-1960s the old rules of the game were modified, and the "old guard" Senators lost much of their earlier influence.

A portion of the change was generational, as the seniority system worked its way and "Young Turks" became "Old Turks." In the 89th Congress, for example, several of the veteran liberals found themselves in choice committee seats, which had previously been denied them. Senators Clark, Pell, and Case were appointed to Foreign Relations; Clark and Pell had lost out two years earlier when a vacancy on that committee was preempted by Senator George A. Smathers (D-Fla.). Senator Quentin N. Burdick (D-N.D.) was given a seat on Judiciary, and Senator Ralph W. Yarborough (D-Tex.) was assigned to Appropriations. Even earlier Proxmire had won his seat on Appropriations.

Meanwhile, a more fundamental transition was under way as the 1962 and 1964 elections brought to the Senate "a group of brainy young liberal newcomers unimpressed with the old rules about the sanctity of seniority."[56] These newcomers included such Democrats as Edward M. Kennedy (Mass.), Joseph Tydings and Daniel B. Brewster (Md.), Birch Bayh (Ind.), Robert F. Kennedy (N.Y.), and Daniel K. Inouye (Hawaii). They have not hesitated to assert their strength when the occasion presented itself. "We don't feel there's time to waste on that old seen-and-not-be-heard business," one of them explained. "After all, if a man manages to get to the Senate, he must have something to contribute."

The rise to prominence of the young liberals, assisted by the Johnson rule on committee assignments, has been accompanied by the aging of many of the conservative leaders. Observers noted that the Southern filibuster on the Voting Rights Act of 1965 was disorganized and somewhat halfhearted; the chief Southern strategist, Senator Russell, was ill and participated very little in the debate. As a staff aide to one Southern leader commented, "They're tired . . . Many of them have been sick. And the civil rights fight [of 1964] really took the heart out of most of them."

Two other factors may have made the way easier for younger Senators wishing to make a reputation for themselves. Within the Democratic party, Majority Leader Mansfield was generally conceded to wield much looser reins than his predecessor, Johnson.

[56] Several of the quotes in this section are drawn from Dan Cordtz, "The Senate Revolution," *Wall Street Journal* (August 6, 1965), p. 8.

"We've had a dispersal of responsibility," Mansfield remarked.
"I'm not the leader, really. They don't do what I tell them. I do
what they tell me."[57] In addition, some of the issues that gained
prominence in the 1960s were those that demanded a sharp,
inquisitive mind rather than the expertise which came from
extended committee tenure. As Senator Thomas H. Kuchel (Calif.),
the Republican Whip, observed, "Now we have things like reapportionment and voting rights—a new man can get his teeth into those
[issues] right away."

With this changed atmosphere, it was understandable that many
younger Senators failed to become enthusiastic for a wholesale rules
revision.[58] The breakdown of the filibuster in civil rights legislation
has no doubt shunted the cloture issue into the background. As one
observer explained, the younger Senators have "discovered what
mostly was lacking was votes—and now they have them." For the
older generation of liberals—Douglas, Clark, Javits, Case, Anderson, Morse, and others—the 89th Congress was a kind of "new
deal" which they had long awaited. Clark himself was led to
conclude: "The old times have changed. The old Senate establishment is gone. Democracy is now pretty much the rule in the
Senate."[59]

The Joint Committee . . . And After

Modern-day congressional reformism is invariably dated from
the Legislative Reorganization Act of 1946. Though the significance
of its actual achievements is debatable, this law envisioned far-
reaching innovations in the reduction of standing committees, the
increase of staff assistance, and the control of fiscal matters. It was
the product of a year of intensive investigations by a Joint
Committee on the Organization of Congress, chaired by Senator

[57] Quoted in *New York Times* (July 17, 1961), p. 11. Under recurrent attack
for his leadership, Mansfield delivered a fascinating reply in *Congressional
Record*, 88th Congress, 1st session, 109 (November 27, 1963), 22857–22866.
For an analysis of Johnson's techniques, see Ralph K. Huitt, "Democratic
Party Leadership in the Senate," *American Political Science Review*, 55
(June 1961), 333–344.

[58] However, the Senate in early 1965 appropriated $80,000 for a Rules Com-
mittee survey of Senate rules.

[59] *Congressional Record*, 89th Congress, 1st session (September 13, 1965,
daily edition), p. 22636.

Robert M. LaFollette, Jr. (Progressive-Wis.) and then-Representative A. S. Mike Monroney (D-Okla.). After 1946, many persons urged creation of a new committee, and in 1963 the Senate Rules Committee reported out such a proposal.[60] As we demonstrated, the joint committee had considerable support among our respondents in the 88th Congress—no doubt in part because it implied no commitment on substantive reform.

On November 25, 1964, Monroney—by then Oklahoma's senior Senator—announced his intention of introducing a resolution in the 89th Congress establishing a successor to the old LaFollette-Monroney Committee. Referring particularly to the appropriations process, Monroney told a news conference that Congress followed "an obsolete system inherited from the Gay Nineties" and compared present procedures to "a group of farmers sitting around a cracker barrel and a pot-bellied stove and trying to run a $100 billion business." In addition to modernizing appropriations, Monroney said that he wanted to study changes in scheduling and in committee structures and workloads.[61] Speaker McCormack, in complying with the DSG's request for a joint committee, designated Representative Ray J. Madden (D-Ind.) to sponsor Monroney's proposal in the House (H. Con. Res. 4). On March 9, the Senate adopted Monroney's plan (S. Con. Res. 2); and two days later, the House approved it by voice vote.

Later named (with Madden) as co-chairman of the committee, Monroney was regarded as the "ideal" sponsor.[62] Because of his role in the 1946 legislation, he is looked to as an elder statesman who stands for "responsible" reform. He is easy-going, universally liked by his colleagues, and the possessor of a "moderate" voting record. His interest in congressional procedure therefore lacks the "programmatic bias" of some members, who in recent years have been conspicuously identified with reformism. In his November announcement, for example, Monroney told reporters:

[60] The measure was an amended version of S. Con. Res. 1, introduced by Senator Clark and 29 co-sponsors and calling for a joint congressional committee. Another plan (S.177), proposed by Senator Case, would have created a mixed commission of members and presidential appointees. The Clark proposal foundered during floor debate when neither he nor Case would accept the Rules Committee's provision preventing the proposed group from recommending changes in Senate or House rules.

[61] Monroney's announcement is reported in *New York Times* (November 26, 1964), p. 42.

[62] *Congressional Quarterly Weekly Report*, 26 (June 25, 1965), 1239.

We will, I hope, not start out with one single purpose to achieve a single objective. Such an approach, or suspicion thereof, has frustrated many well-intentioned efforts of the past to modernize Congress.

Elaborating on the "efficiency" motif, Monroney stresses the need for "modernizing" Congress. He believes that an incremental approach is essential to attract the votes needed to adopt reforms; he points out, for example, that the 1946 Act was approved in part because it was accompanied by a pay-raise bill desired by most members.

Many reformers, especially from the liberal camp, find this approach too cautious. The difference in strategy came to the surface during the brief but spirited Senate floor debate over the Monroney proposal. According to Monroney's resolution, the new joint committee—like its 1945 predecessor—was to be barred from making recommendations for changes in House or Senate rules. Monroney argued that a successful reorganization effort should avoid contentious rules fights—as over the Senate cloture rule. "The intent of this resolution," he told the Senate, "is to seek solutions to the problems of Congress on which there is a consensus that something should be done."[63] Although many changes would obviously involve the rules (for example, committee jurisdictions), such alterations could be stimulated by the joint committee's work —as in 1945–1946—and then processed separately by the two houses. A fine sense of proprieties influenced Monroney to observe the constitutional provision that each house be the judge of its own rules, although he noted that the joint committee would not be prohibited from hearing testimony on the rules.

A few Senators—including Clark, Case, Morse, and Javits— charged that reorganization would be meaningful only if the committee were free to investigate what Clark called "our present iniquitous rules." During the floor debate Clark declared: "I find myself unable to agree that the resolution as he [Monroney] has caused it to be drawn would accomplish what the body of the resolution purports to do." Those men who drafted the resolution, he continued, "do not wish to put their support behind any investigation . . . which might conceivably overthrow the balance

---

[63] *Congressional Record*, 89th Congress, 1st session (March 8, 1965, daily edition), p. 4236. The ensuing debate is found in pp. 4223–4429 (March 8–9).

of power in the Senate . . ." Clark estimated that three fourths of
"the work which the committee ought to do" would be barred by
the exclusion of consideration of the rules. Clark himself had
introduced no less than 27 specific rules changes the previous
session, and ". . . not one of these . . . could be the subject of
recommendation by the joint committee under the resolution of the
Senator from Oklahoma." Clark's move to include rules within the
joint committee's jurisdiction was defeated by a 58–29 roll-call
vote.

The joint committee's 12 members—three from each house for
each party—illustrated once again the intricate political considerations interwoven with congressional innovation. The members were
named by the majority and minority leaders in the two houses.
Monroney, who headed the six-man Senate delegation, was acceptable to conservatives as well as to most liberals. Though initially
somewhat reluctant to serve, Madden was the Speaker's designee to
lead the House delegation; he was chosen as a liberal and a member
of the House Rules Committee, which would have to pass on the
joint committee's proposals. Representative Richard Bolling (D-
Mo.) was also a member of Rules and was more predominently
identified with reform than Madden; but Bolling had opposed
McCormack's succession to the Speakership, had written a book
containing critical references to McCormack,[64] and in any event was
unacceptable to conservatives. From the Senate, Case was named to
the committee but Clark was passed over. The only House delegate
with a long-standing expressed interest in reorganization was
Representative Thomas B. Curtis (R-Mo.). Other members rounded
out the ideological balance of the group: from the Senate, John J.
Sparkman (D-Ala.), Lee Metcalf (D-Mont.), Karl E. Mundt (R-
S.D.), and J. Caleb Boggs (R-Del.) ; and from the House, Jack
Brooks (D-Tex.), Ken Hechler (D-W.Va.), Robert P. Griffin (R-
Mich.), and Durward G. Hall (R-Mo.). It is relevant to note that
every Senator had served in the House and that every committee
member—except for Monroney—was up for reelection in 1966.

Choice of the committee's four professional staff aides was
parceled among the four delegations. Monroney designated W.
DeVier Pierson, a young Oklahoma attorney, as chief counsel;
House Democrats picked the only political scientist to serve on the

---

[64] See Bolling's *House Out of Order* (New York: E. P. Dutton, 1965), esp.
pp. 72ff.

staff—Nicholas A. Masters of Pennsylvania State University. The
House Republicans selected former Representative George Meader
(R-Mich.); their Senate colleagues chose Melvin W. Sneed, an
experienced congressional staff aide. An expenditure ceiling of
$150,000 was placed on the committee's work through January 31,
1966, but a supplementary appropriation was made later to allow
the committee to complete its work.[65]

On May 10, 1965, the joint committee initiated its series of public
hearings. Forty-one public sessions were held during the next four
months in the Old Supreme Court Chamber of the Capitol
Building; testimony was gathered from 83 members of Congress, 19
political scientists, 26 interest-group spokesmen, and nine government officials—a total of 137 witnesses. In addition, several busi-
ness- and management-consultant firms briefed members and staff
on management techniques and on automated data storage and
retrieval systems. A summary of the types of proposals covered by
the hearings appears in Table 5.2.

Fiscal processes loomed large in the committee hearings. The topic
was discussed by all three committee chairmen who testified—
Senators Warren G. Magnuson (D-Wash.) and John L. McClellan
(D-Ark.) and Representative George H. Mahon (D-Texas); and the
only major executive-branch witness, Budget Director Charles L.
Schultze, described the implications of the Administration's new
program-budgeting techniques. Housekeeping matters, floor procedures, committee work, and improvements in scheduling were also
discussed; and some members professed to be intrigued by the
proposal from Senator Clark, Representative Frank Chelf (D-Ky.),
and others for four-year terms for Congressmen. "I think just
about every reasonable and constructive idea for the reorganization
of Congress—plus a few silly ones—is in our files," Monroney
said.[66]

Monroney determined to wind up the committee's work in 1966,
so that its recommendations could be acted upon before the close of
the 89th Congress. The House and Senate contingents of the
committee would attempt to be appointed as select committees of
their respective houses in order to get the recommendations
accepted and incorporated into the rules. Few observers expected

[65] The American Political Science Association's extensive "Study of
Congress" was, unfortunately, not completed in time to provide a supplement
to the committee's own research.

[66] Cited by Cabell Phillips in *New York Times* (August 31, 1965), p. 13.

TABLE 5.2

Reforms Proposed during Hearings
of the Joint Committee on the
Organization of the Congress, 1965

Category	Number*
Fiscal controls	83
Scheduling and floor procedures	43
Information and research	39
Committee meetings and hearings	29
Committee jurisdiction	27
Elections and campaigns	25
Committee staffing	24
Office staff and allowances	22
Housekeeping functions	22
Committee chairmen	21
Oversight	18
Electronic aids	17
Ethics	16
Party leadership	10
Committee assignments	9
Foreign policy	8
Nonlegislative workload	7
Subcommittees	6
TOTAL	426

* The numbers represent distinct proposals by witnesses during 41 days of hearings (May 10—September 23, 1965). But the numbers do not necessarily represent the number of witnesses; in many instances, a proposal was endorsed or opposed by more than one witness. Compiled from U.S. Congress, Joint Committee on the Organization of the Congress, *Second Interim Report* (S. Rept. 948, 89th Congress, 2nd session, 1966), pp. 7–29.

any startling innovations, and indeed Monroney's own philosophy seemed to foreclose sweeping changes. As *Congressional Quarterly* surveyed the situation,

> . . . it would be unrealistic to expect much in the way of recommendations for far-reaching reforms. What . . . appears most likely is that the committee may confine itself to those proposals that would be least upsetting to the established order and most acceptable to Congress as a whole, such as provisions for more services and staff.[67]

[67] *Congressional Quarterly Weekly Report,* 26 (June 25, 1965), 1240.

No doubt the pessimism of outside observers stemmed from the widely accepted ideology of reformism, which tends to dismiss as trivial those changes that do not abolish the filibuster or the seniority system. But our analysis has shown the difficulty of isolating ''far-reaching'' reforms from the trivial. One of the first joint committee's most far-reaching innovations, a reduction in the number of standing committees, was introduced as an efficiency-oriented reform but became significant because, by reducing the ratio of ''Chiefs'' to ''Indians,'' it heightened the prerogatives of the seniority leaders. Similarly, the 1965 joint committee may well introduce seemingly trivial reforms that are actually far-reaching. Limitations on committee assignments or central (that is, majority-party leadership) control of scheduling of committee meetings and hearings—two innovations discussed by the joint committee—could have an impact far beyond their stated objective of regularizing the congressional workload.

Moreover, the joint committee could hasten the adoption of many so-called ''marginal'' changes which would have the effect of smoothing congressional operations and making the Congressman's life more orderly. The committee's broad ideological mixture (and, perhaps, the fact that all its members had House service) would undoubtedly render its proposals more palatable to the legislators. In such circumstances, there was something to be said for Monroney's incrementalist approach. ''A lot of little reforms add up to a big reform,'' he remarked during one of the hearings. ''If we are going to get an up-to-date, modern Congress, it will be a mosaic you build from lots of little improvements.''[68]

Conclusions

The innovations occasioned by the 89th Congress illustrate the varied and discontinuous course of reform. Broadly speaking, two types of structural innovation are evident in our narrative: first, those relatively noncontroversial changes designed to increase the ''efficiency'' of the institution; and second, those innovations aimed at enhancing the position of party or policy blocs. In both of these general groupings of reform activity were the specific innovations that conformed to various theories of congressional functioning and

---

[68] *Joint Committee Hearings* (1965), Part I, p. 75.

promised diverse (though not always predictable) consequences for the operation of the institution.

The "noncontroversial" reforms are typified by the several Senate rules changes in 1963–1964 and by the creation of the Joint Committee on the Organization of the Congress in 1965. Such innovations are usually pressed by legislators, typified by Senator Monroney, who desire to make congressional operations more expeditious and more tolerable for the participants. Though the efficiency motif was predominant in the joint committee's deliberations, an accompanying theme was that the proposed reforms might strengthen Congress in its policy struggles with the executive. Given the pervasiveness of the notion of congressional supremacy among legislators, this argument no doubt won over a number of members who would otherwise have been uninterested in the reforms. It is relevant to note, however, that such noncontroversial reforms are seldom neutral in their impact upon the internal congressional power structure. A classic example is the consolidation of committees effected by the Legislative Reorganization Act of 1946.

The other type of reform is exemplified by the Senate cloture fight, the Republicans' minority staffing drive, and the House 21-day rule. All of them arise directly from party or factional struggles. Most of the reform activity described in this chapter is of this type. The ferment within the Democratic congressional parties during the 1950s and 1960s represented the efforts of liberal and urban members to pry their legislative program from the more conservative congressional power structure (loosely defined as the "establishment"). If we were to characterize this struggle in terms of differences among purposive roles, we might view it as a quarrel between "Inventor" types, who want to "get things done," and "Ritualists," who are more concerned with the value of established procedures for doing them. In the Senate, the growing liberal majority appeared to have established itself without recourse to formal alterations in procedures. Indeed, their increased ability to realize their goals seemed to dissipate their interest in changing formal rules. In the larger and more hierarchical House, the adoption of several high-priority rules changes was required to ratify the dominant position of the liberals in the 89th Congress. Consensus on substantial changes was not easily obtained within these blocs, or even within the relatively homogeneous and reform-minded Democratic Study Group.

162 CHAPTER FIVE

The reforms pressed by the liberal Democrats typically conformed in a surprising degree to the party-government model of congressional functions—even though not many of these reformers would accept the assumptions or implications of party-government theory. The reason for the prevalence of the party-government theme is historical. Believing themselves the dominant wing of their party, the liberal reformers naturally sought means for bringing dissident congressional leaders into line with the party's national platform and program. Hence, the DSG reformers attempted explicitly to strengthen the role of the party majority and its elective leadership against certain of the more conservative seniority leaders, who tended to stray off the reservation. To the extent that the position of the party nationally tends to be upheld by the President, these reforms contain a subordinate theme of executive force—although, as we have seen, even the President's strongest congressional supporters tend to reject this interpretation.

A parallel conflict was experienced among House Republicans. Inventive and party-minded Republicans of varying ideological persuasions labored during the early 1960s to strengthen their party's voice through policy committees, increased staffing on committees, and the election of "attractive" leaders. Their purpose was to develop and publicize Republican alternatives to the majority party's programs. Though the ideological cleavage was apparently not as severe as within the Democratic party, many of the more senior Republicans were clearly unenthusiastic over these innovations.

To many outside observers, the changes adopted in the 89th Congress appear inadequate to remedy the fundamental ills of the institution. Advocates of the literary theory, as well as frustrated congressional Republicans, believe that Congress is falling further under the shadow of the Presidency. While considerably mollified by the work of the "fabulous 89th," some liberal reformers also remain uneasy about the future of Congress. A *New York Times* editorial writer, for example, declared that "if Congress is ever to overcome the minority vetoes, tedious delays and irresponsibility of the present procedure, reforms will have to come."[69] It is clear that the 89th Congress, no matter how reform minded it may have considered itself, had not put out the fires of discontent over congressional performance.

[69] William V. Shannon, "Congress: Reform Still Needed," *New York Times* (September 6, 1965), p. 14.

CONCLUSION: INVENTION, INCREMENTALISM, AND THE FUTURE OF CONGRESS

As Congress approaches the end of its second century, it is the object of continuous debate and examination. In a sense this attention is entirely appropriate, for legislative bodies are intensely political institutions that are both visible and accessible. Many of the attacks upon Congress are the result of conflicting political demands and may be expected to subside when the institution, in response to electoral or representational processes, succeeds in absorbing or resolving the controversy.

Such a cycle apparently occurred in the early 1960s. After almost a decade of relative political calm, an activist Administration began to fill the congressional agenda with a variety of legislative initiatives. When the temporary stalemate of 1963 was surmounted, the so-called "fabulous 89th" Congress became so "successful" that by late 1965 it appeared to enjoy even greater popularity than the President. A politically responsive Congress can hopefully ride out similar periods of conflict in the future.

Yet the depth and pervasiveness of the debate over Congress transcends the temporary cyclical changes in the level of political conflict. Widely shared fears for the future of Congress are heightened by the awareness that this century is generally considered an anti-parliamentary era—that legislatures in many nations are walking corpses, which have survived in form but not in political vitality. And these fears are compounded by fundamental and long-standing philosophic differences about the appropriate

functions of the national legislature. The dilemma posed by these
differences is not insoluble, but it constitutes the essence of the
present "parliamentary crisis" in America.

The Incremental Nature of Change

Change is a part of any functioning institution. Whether the
result of broad consensus or the hard-won struggle of a relatively
small faction, whether planned or unplanned, whether designed to
accomplish bold new purposes or to maintain traditional functions
in the face of a new environment, change must be the concern of all
participants in an ongoing political institution. Conservatives no
less than reformers must involve themselves with the problem of
change.

Obviously, changes can and do occur in the absence of participant agreement on goals, problems, and means-ends relationships.
Innovations must take place in the context of an active institution
where powerful interests are at stake. The participants in that institution cannot afford the luxury of that useful fiction, the *tabula
rasa*, in devising reform. Even the Founding Fathers were constrained to work from blueprints of existing institutions in England
and the Colonies and to calculate with sensitivity the political interests with which their institutions were built to contend.[1] Nor
could they be at all certain of the consequences of their innovations.

Contemporary innovators enjoy even less maneuverability. The
Congressmen who were demanding reform in the 89th Congress
were restrained by political exigencies. The leaders of the Democratic Study Group, for example, were explicitly concerned with
developing a package that would attract votes and enhance their
record of success. Nor were these reformers themselves in full
agreement: their disarray on the discharge petition caused them to
abandon that proposal, and their philosophy of change, embodied
by the measures they agreed upon, was by no means clear.

The Joint Committees on the Organization of Congress also
worked in the context of compromise. The 1946 Legislative Reorganization Act was supported by Congressmen with widely divergent perspectives and motivations and with many differing concep-
tions of the kind of reform that would result from its adoption. The

---

[1] See John P. Roche, "The Founding Fathers: A Reform Caucus in
Action," *American Political Science Review*, 55 (December 1961), 799–816.

1965 joint committee proceeded similarly under Co-Chairman Monroney's explicit view that reform is "a mosaic you build from lots of little improvements."

Some of the most fundamental changes in congressional operations have occurred without the awareness of most of the participants. For example, the President's role as an initiator of and lobbyist for legislation has been the result of a gradual enlargement of presidential power, some of which probably escaped the notice of even the staunchest defenders of congressional prerogatives. Richard Neustadt has termed it "among the quietest pragmatic innovations in our constitutional history." He relates, for instance, that until the Kennedy administration the fiction was maintained that Presidents themselves did not present draft bills embodying their legislative recommendations. The so-called "Administration" bills were given by agencies to friendly legislators for introduction "by request." After 1961, however, draft bills began to accompany Presidential messages sent to the Speaker and President of the Senate over the signature of the President; and no one noticed the change. The fact that "no one noticed" was the most striking aspect of this silent constitutional revolution that has been taking place over the last two generations.[2] It is the relatively recent awareness of this shift to the executive that has led so many commentators of differing political persuasions to conclude that "something must be done about Congress."

The proponents of the literary theory, who are most enthusiastic about the functions Congress has traditionally performed, are disturbed over the current state of affairs; and some have proposed far-reaching redirections of congressional activities. On the other hand, the developments of the past generation have not completely satisfied the advocates of executive force, who believe that radical changes are necessary if Congress is to mesh its activities with those of the executive establishment. The party-government advocates, too, have their proposals for altering the structure and functions of Congress. Obviously, the prescriptive aspects of these theories are associated with basically different philosophical premises, policy preferences, and definitions of the situation.

In few "real world" situations are the actors able to analyze

---

[2] Richard Neustadt, "Politicians and Bureaucracy," *The Congress and America's Future*, ed. David B. Truman (Englewood Cliffs, N.J.: Prentice-Hall, 1965), pp. 110–111.

their motives, examine all the alternatives, calculate the effects, and innovate with the guidance of clearly specified goals. And even if feasible, comprehensive innovation would be extremely hazardous in a going political system. Full knowledge of the intent and probable consequences of change might invite defeat by laying bare the underlying disagreements surrounding the proper role of Congress.

For all of these reasons, it is understandable that much of the development of Congress as an institution is traced through changes that are marginal and gradual in character. Does this mean that in the future Congress is destined to respond haphazardly to limited structural problems that arise? Or are there ways of expanding the scope of rationality in successfully "muddling through" the institutional crisis?

Guidelines for Strategists of Change

Notwithstanding the incremental and sometimes even "accidental" character of institutional innovation, individuals are confronted from time to time with at least limited opportunities for deliberate action. Our concern thus far has been to describe and interpret some of the political features that affect stability and change in Congress. By implication our analysis suggests some strategies that might be selected for moving from what is to what might be in the complex maze of legislative politics. At the very least, our findings provide guidelines that will give perspective to those who seek to change our national legislature.

Presumably, these guidelines can be translated into political discussion as a set of "givens," which can be understood, accepted, and applied by Representatives, Senators, and nonparticipant observers. We are attempting not to prescribe the directions that congressional change should take but merely to alert the traveler to the signposts in the intricate landscape of reform politics.

The following guidelines were most readily extractable from our descriptive analysis and, we believe, meet the conditions just set forth.

1. PROBABLE POLITICAL CONSEQUENCES

Any proposed change should be examined closely for its likely political effects and not simply for its conformity to an orderly theory. Some current practices that seem irrational may be highly defensible in political terms. The would-be reformer must first understand the political functions or dysfunctions of existing procedures. Second, he must show either that modifications of current procedures will serve these functions more faithfully or that the functions themselves are expendable. Third, he ought to be reasonably certain that the proposed reform will yield the desired result X rather than undesired results Y or Z. An illustration of these considerations is found in the discussion on the use of electronic voting devices.

Political scientists are particularly attracted to proposals that conform to an organization-chart notion of congressional operations —without regard to the actual political effects of their proposals. To paraphrase Chief Justice John Marshall, we must never forget that it is a *legislature* we are expounding. The political effects of a given innovation are never perfectly knowable; but Congressmen and Senators are aware that they must try to calculate these effects; and political scientists ought to be prepared to give them realistic assistance in predicting the consequences of institutional innovations.

Of course, the shrewd reformer will carefully consider his tactics in communicating and publicizing the expected results of his reforms. In the world of politics, agreement is often reached only because the individuals concerned fail to understand fully the consequences of their decisions. "Clarity" and "understanding," as we have already noted, may lead as readily to fear and hostility as to agreement. But the basic admonition remains: a reformer must attempt to insure that the proposed innovations are ultimately consistent with his own designs; it is then a tactical decision how much he wishes to broadcast the expected results.

2. ANALYZING THE "REFORM MARKET"

The resources that can be expended to bring about change are invariably limited. Hence, a knowledge of the "reform market" will direct the reformer's attention toward some changes and away from others. Our own findings provide some rather crude measures of sentiment on a number of typical proposals; other changes can be tested by "counting the House" in a similar manner. Further, it may even be possible to fashion new reform proposals by building upon known attitudes and preferences of Congressmen.

Despite the divergent views on roles, problems, and outcomes expressed by their proponents, several specific reforms enjoyed more support than opposition in the House of Representatives during the 88th Congress. Increased personal and committee staffing was a conspicuous example. A balance of support also existed for the policy of assigning larger minority staffs to committees, even though this favorable majority was composed of Representatives who were in sharp disagreement on many other matters.[3] Other measures supported by a majority of the respondents included scheduling more time for committee work at the beginning of annual sessions, the formal adoption of year-long congressional sessions with provision for scheduled recesses, and the publicizing of committee votes.[4] But in predicting the likelihood of adoption, our respondents felt that only five of the 32 reforms covered by our survey had at least a fifty-fifty chance of adoption by the House in the coming decade. The Congressmen were optimistic about authorizing an Administrative Assistant for each Congressman, establishing a committee to study congressional reorganization, creating a Joint Committee on Fiscal Policy, holding year-long sessions, and broadcasting committee hearings.[5]

Other changes that received majority assent in our study might win House adoption if they were presented under propitious circumstances. Both the four-year term and the reestablishment of the 21-day rule enjoyed a balance of support during the 88th Congress, but both were judged by most members to have only a small chance of adoption. Yet the 21-day rule was reinstated at the beginning of the 89th Congress, and the prospect for acceptance of the four-year term was somewhat enhanced with the surprise endorsement of that measure by President Johnson in his 1966 State of the Union message.

The change in the political status of these two measures is a reminder of some important factors that condition the politics of reform. When election results change significantly the party and seniority composition of Congress, the status of reorganization proposals that divide members according to party and/or seniority may be substantially altered. And in the unlikely event that the strength of noncongressional pressures for reform is substantially

---

[3] See Appendix B, Table B-1, proposal 10.

[4] See Appendix B, Table B-1, proposals 4, 6, and 13.

[5] See Appendix B, Table B-1, proposals 2, 3, 5, 6, and 11.

increased, Congress—or at least some of its members—can be expected to evidence increased optimism and renewed interest in change. Finally, legislators may well be conservative in lending their support to reform proposals prior to the time for formal commitment. In the absence of adequate information about the support for a given reform, many members apparently assume that their colleagues (particularly the leadership) "would never stand for it." When a reasonable innovation is formally presented to Congress and "true" preferences become better known, reform-minded Congressmen may be pleasantly surprised at the "snowball effect" that could result.

Member acceptance is probably the most salient requirement of congressional change. Outside observers can afford to engage in outspoken agitation or in utopian thinking; indeed, a healthy political dialogue implies that some people somewhere are saying outrageous things. But reformist Congressmen must be concerned with the economy of their efforts; they must measure the desirability of various changes against the costs of obtaining favorable votes.

We are not—let us emphasize—stating that the only good changes are those that can win votes; nor are we discounting the long-run effect of educational campaigns in altering attitudes. (Some thoughtful reformers, in fact, may be willing to forfeit the hope of immediate results in exchange for the long-run benefits to be obtained from assuming a radical stance.) But it is essential to recognize the limitations to reform imposed by the attitudes of Congressmen.

3. COUNTERCYCLICAL BEHAVIOR

A basic problem in generating support for change is the tendency for Congress is to be judged according to its performance at a given moment. Much reform energy is wasted because agitation among members (and outsiders) tends to be greatest when policy conflicts are most intense. When the issues are resolved (with or without institutional change), the concern over modifying the structure abates. Thus, at a time when there is consensus within the legislature there is little pressure to effectuate change. The spasm of reform at the beginning of the 89th Congress was the reaction of a "new" majority to the accumulated frustrations from the stalemates of previous sessions. Yet as the legislative blueprints for the "Great

Society'' were approved with unprecedented alacrity, ''the voice of would-be reformers,'' as *Newsweek* put it, ''was effectively silenced because, in the public eye, Congress [had] reformed itself.''[6]

The activist who chooses to press for congressional reform in a time of relative political calm must, in a sense, labor doubly hard to excite reformist sentiment. Yet the possibilities for change in periods of minimal conflict must not be dismissed. A temporary reduction in the level of conflict on Capitol Hill may well release some of the time, energy, and political resources of enough Congressmen to permit the study—and perhaps support—of changes in congressional organization and procedure. To break away from the dilemmas for reform imposed by the cycles of political controversy, Congress should provide for its own institutionalized means of ''preventive maintenance.'' If Congressmen are indeed self-conscious about their position in the American political system, they might consider whether the stakes involved do not justify more than one major self-appraisal every generation. Much could be gained by creating a permanent body on the lines of the La Follette-Monroney and Monroney-Madden Joint Committees on the Organization of the Congress. In a sense, the future role of Congress rests upon the ability of that institution to stimulate continuous and critical thinking about change—before change is forced upon it.

Epilogue: A Modest Polemic on Political Gamesmanship

The purpose of our research has been to describe and analyze the dynamics of congressional innovation. In one sense, we have achieved this purpose simply in reporting our findings and suggesting their implications. But in another sense, we are only now in a position to approach the problem of recommending congressional change by applying our general knowledge to the complexities of innovative behavior. To be sure, there is nothing in our research that can actually recommend to us the content of specific reforms. Anything further we say, therefore, must stem more from personal values than from analysis of data.

It would be presumptuous for us to suggest that we can define the

6 *Newsweek* (January 17, 1966), p. 18.

precise relationship between a given innovation and the quality or power of a future Congress; indeed, we have repeatedly stressed the difficulties of such a total rationality. But, as we observed in the introduction to this study, it is instructive for scholars to devote some of their attention to such matters. What kind of a Congress is it that we want? What needs to be done to achieve such a Congress?

We suggest that the maximization of opportunities for free competition of interests and values should be a prime value in thinking about the future of Congress. This tenet is a most familiar one in democratic theory: John Stuart Mill, for example, wrote of the "marketplace of ideas," and Charles E. Lindblom has pointed out the desirability of a system through which semiautonomous political actors can freely adjust to one another. We would apply this concept to the problem of Congress by arguing that organization and procedure should insure that no political interest making demands upon the national legislature is permanently or severely deprived of the opportunity to achieve its goals.[7]

We do not mean to suggest that all interests, no matter how small or extreme, will have an equal chance for success. However, barriers to such interests should be embodied not in congressional structure but rather in the good sense of the American people and their representatives. That is to say, congressional rules should not consistently predetermine the outcomes of the numerous conflicts that infuse vitality into American politics. This competition should be valid not only for conflict arising from intellectual or economic or geographic interests, but also for conflict between institutionally based groups—incumbent versus challenger, senior versus junior member, majority versus minority party, Senate versus House, and executive versus Congress. Reform proposals should be rejected if they give inordinate advantage to one or more of these groups. Although it is difficult for a preponderant legislative majority to show restraint at all times, this "rule of the game" should be consistently articulated and acknowledged.

The criterion of freedom of competition ought to imply that the rules of a legislative body are available to anyone who can utilize them. But the *New York Times*, commenting editorially in mid-1965

---

[7] At minimum, "almost any value that any even relatively small number of citizens moderately or strongly wishes to see weighed into the policy-making process will be weighed in at some value significantly above zero." Charles E. Lindblom, *The Intelligence of Democracy* (New York: Free Press of Glencoe, 1965), p. 239.

upon a complex procedural maneuver in the House, managed to praise the Democratic floor leadership for exploiting the 21-day rule to its limits while at the same time expressing righteous indignation over the Rules Committee's shrewd use of *its* prerogatives. The basis for this distinction, of course, was the *Times'* judgment that the objectives of the leadership were "worthwhile" while those of the Rules Committee were "irresponsible."[8] Legislators themselves are equally myopic. Some Senators have contended that one method of exploiting the rules—the filibuster—is acceptable while another method—cloture—is not. Such uneven judgments are the result of the universal propensity to identify rectitude and legitimacy with one's own side of a controversy. However, it should be clear that once a rule or procedure has been established in a legislative body, the legitimacy of its use by any participant should not be questioned.

Extending the principle of healthy competition to the interplay between governmental institutions illuminates the attractiveness of the literary theory, which emphasizes the benefits of at least a semblance of balance between the executive and legislative branches. Advocates of the literary theory do not deny variations over time and from issue to issue in the precise sharing of functions and relative levels of influence between the branches. But the minimal condition of the literary theory is the opportunity for either branch to regain lost prerogatives or to acquire compensatory functions. The theory is clearly hostile to a system that would endow either branch with a steady or irreversible increase of functions and authority at the expense of the other branch. We have pointed out frequently that it is the legislature which is currently experiencing the more profound difficulties in the political tug of war. But we believe also that the present situation offers a number of opportunities for Congress to redefine its constitutional position.

Strict application of the literary formula, however, is clearly out of the question in contemporary America. Congress is no longer the chief maker of laws in our political system; it no longer enjoys a monopoly in initiating policy proposals, determining their broad outlines, or even assigning them priority on the legislative agenda. This task has now passed largely—though by no means totally—to

---

[8] Editorial, "Black Monday," *New York Times* (September 15, 1965), p. 42.

the President and the executive establishment. (Not that Congress has ceased to be a seedbed of ideas: indeed, great portions of the "New Frontier" and "Great Society" programs had their origins on Capitol Hill.) Senators and Congressmen may be said to lobby for the inclusion of proposals in the President's program and to negotiate over details of the proposals; but almost invariably executive-branch technicians formulate the detailed provisions, and the President and his advisors determine the emphasis and the timing. For the historical reasons cited by the executive-force theorists, it does not seem likely that Congress can perform the lawmaking function as it is implied by the Constitution.

Although we cannot accept the literary theory's specific delineation of functions, we nevertheless accept its fundamental premise— the principle of "gamesmanship" inherent in the constitutional notion of balanced powers. If the traditional lawmaking functions —deliberation especially, but also representation and consensus building—are no longer the preeminent domain of Congress, what functions remain through which it can best make its own unique contribution to policy making and justify its place as an equal partner in the political process? Broadly speaking, the remaining tasks are four: legitimization, policy clarification, oversight, and constituent service. We shall consider each briefly in turn.

Legitimization denotes the invocation of the symbols of a democratic legislature to encourage acceptance of policy outcomes. Although this is a positive function, its opposite is also implied: the power to withhold legitimacy—Burnham's power of the ultimate "No!" The legislature's veto power is functional because legitimization is more meaningful if it is not automatically or freely bestowed. But even more critically, the entire notion of the legislature as an autonomous body rests upon its ability to withhold approval from an Administration's initiatives. By this form of "blackmail," Congress can make itself heard.

At the level of the individual legislator, this "blackmail" is possible because a member's vote is not foreordained; rather, in many instances, it must be "bought." The ultimate power of the legislative veto, therefore, forces an Administration to bargain with members individually and with Congress collectively. The vitality with which other congressional functions can be pursued therefore rests in large part on the existence of this veto power.

Policy clarification is the task of giving visibility and publicity to problems and issues. In this task, Congress labors at a severe disadvantage when compared to the Presidency. Yet there are frequent instances in which persistent legislators have succeeded in closing the "visibility gap." This success may be the result of an individual member's long-term obsession with a particular problem: for example, a John Moss on administrative secrecy, an Edward Long on governmental invasions of privacy, or a J. William Fulbright on foreign-policy myths. Or it may be the result of a series of spectacular hearings—like Estes Kefauver's celebrated inquiries into organized crime or drug prices. In any event, the public is sorely in need of alternative sources of information in this era of inevitable news management by private and public bureaucracies. A Congress that encourages responsible publicity entrepreneurship among its membership can perform an essential public service.

With regard to the federal bureaucracy, Congress ought to provide the "continuous watchfulness" specified by the Legislative Reorganization Act of 1946. Unfortunately, too few committees have fulfilled this responsibility; the reasons for this failure would themselves comprise a lengthy study. The success of the oversight function rests upon the ability and willingness of Congress to impose sanctions upon noncompliant agencies. Nor is oversight usually confined to a general review of policy implementation; in fact, it often begins with haggling on specific cases and proceeds from that point to a consideration of necessary statutory revisions.

The final task, constituent service, is often denigrated by observers of Congress and sometimes by members themselves. In his "errand boy" role, a Congressman serves as liaison and special advocate for constituents having dealings with federal bureaus or agencies. Many people contend that legislators should not "waste time" on such matters (despite the fact that staff personnel may take over as large or as small a portion of this load as a member wishes). Yet, with the government's increasing involvement in our daily lives, citizens are more than ever in need of assistance in dealing with governmental agencies. Why not have legislators stand ready to perform this service? First, it is a convenient method for a member to build credit with his constituents. Secondly, his appeals on behalf of constituents are likely to be more effective because he is an elected legislator whose support the Administration must bargain for. And finally, constituent casework can help a member identify problems that demand review or statutory solution. Some routinization of constituent services (for example, through a

centralized, congressionally controlled Office of Administrative
Counsel) might be desirable, but only so long as Senators and
Representatives themselves remained in close touch with the pro-
cess.

In performing these four tasks, Congressmen face the problem of
equipping themselves to participate successfully in what has been
termed the "game against nature"—the struggle to apply at least a
modicum of rationality to decision making in a society of increasing
complexity. Perfect rationality in decision making is, of course,
unattainable; nor should legislators simply duplicate executive-
branch specialization in their effort to make professional judgments
on technical questions. Indeed, the legislator's unique contribution
to decision making may be not so much his technical expertise as his
political sense—his feel for the strains and tolerances of the
political system. Yet Congress does have a serious problem in
obtaining adequate technical information. Four out of every five
Congressmen told us that "lack of information" and "complexity
of decision making" were major problems preventing them from
performing as effectively as they wished. Satisfying this need,
therefore, is a major task of congressional reorganization.[9]

The thread that runs through the tasks we have enumerated may
be characterized as follows: Congress must help to supply disson-
ance, or opposition, in public decision making. One of the most
important commodities Congress can provide is an institutional
base for alternative viewpoints and criticisms. Thus, steps should be
taken to increase the probability that Congress will act independently—that it will possess both the inclination and the influence to
function as an autonomous voice in the affairs of state. Internally,
this viewpoint suggests that Congress be structured as pluralistically
as possible, so that policy entrepreneurship by individuals, committees, voting blocs, and parties themselves will be maximized. All in
all, we are, to borrow a phrase from Lindblom, arguing for
"permitting legislators and executives to act flexibly and intelligently toward each other and in interchange with the citizenry in
order to explore . . . all possible opportunities for agreement and
acceptable aggregation."[10]

Finally, we wish to make it clear that while we are dissatisfied

[9] On this problem, see the testimony of James A. Robinson in *Joint
Committee Hearings* (1965), Part V, pp. 783ff; and *Management Study of the
U.S. Congress* (Arthur D. Little, Inc., 1965).

[10] Lindblom, p. 319.

with the quality of the criticism of Congress, we believe it altogether appropriate that our national legislature remain a center of controversy. For Congress is uniquely the people's own place, and differences should legitimately arise over its methods of operation. When congressional functioning ceases to be a matter of contention, it may be a signal that the legislative body is no longer worth arguing about. Crisis as well as consensus is the hallmark of democratic politics. As Fisher Ames once remarked, democracy, as a form of politics, resembles a crude wooden raft: it is exceedingly difficult to sink, but one's feet are always wet.

APPENDIXES

A.

A METHODOLOGICAL NOTE ON THE SAMPLE SURVEY OF THE HOUSE OF REPRESENTATIVES

Much of the data presented in Chapters 3 and 4 was derived from personal interviews with members of the House of Representatives in the 88th Congress (1963–1964). This survey was prompted by the lack of systematic information concerning congressional views of (1) the normative and enacted roles of Congress and Congressmen, (2) the problems of Congress and its members, (3) the proposed reforms of Congress, and (4) the politics of congressional reorganization. That such an undertaking might be both fruitful and feasible was suggested by the role-oriented research on state legislatures undertaken by John C. Wahlke and his associates and by the success of James A. Robinson and of Warren E. Miller and Donald E. Stokes in their attempts to interview sizable samples of members of Congress by means of structured survey instruments.[1]

Description of Samples

A number of considerations—both practical and theoretical—persuaded us to limit our survey to the House of Representatives. First, previous personal experience and the observations of other

---

[1] John C. Wahlke, Heinz Eulau, William Buchanan, and LeRoy C. Ferguson, *The Legislative System* (New York: John Wiley, 1962); James A. Robinson, *Congress and Foreign Policy-Making* (Homewood, Illinois: Dorsey Press, 1962); Warren E. Miller and Donald E. Stokes, ''Constituency Influence in Congress,'' *American Political Science Review*, 57 (March 1963), 45–56.

students of Congress suggested to us that Representatives would be more accessible to scholars than Senators. This inaccessibility of Senators is explained in part by their higher status, by the greater bureaucratization of their offices (which means that more assistants must be bypassed before one may see the principals), and by what may well be objectively busier senatorial schedules.

Second, the anticipated use of multivariate analytical techniques required that our sample size approach, if not exceed, 100 cases; and the available financial resources limited our sample to about that figure. To have included Senate interviews in a sample of such modest size would have precluded analysis of attitudes internal to each house—that is, it would have forced us to ignore what we presumed would be a very important institutional variable.

Within the House of Representatives, three samples of members were developed. The first of these we have referred to as the "general" sample. This sample consisted of 87 completed interviews that were stratified by party and by leadership position within the party in such fashion that (1) the completed sample had the same ratio of Democrats to Republicans as the House as a whole; and (2) the proportion of leaders and of nonleaders interviewed (within each party group) was the same as that actually existing in the House.[2] Respondents appropriate to each of these four groups (Democratic and Republican leaders and nonleaders) were selected on a random basis from a list of all members of the House.

Because we assumed that leadership position (and the closely associated seniority variable) would be critical in the analysis of the politics of reform, and because our general sample contained an appropriately small number of formal leaders, we interviewed an additional 23 members holding leadership positions. This randomly drawn "leadership oversample," when combined with the general-sample respondents holding leadership positions, provided us with enough cases to permit analysis of differences in attitudes within the House leadership group.

---

[2] Those members classified as leaders were respondents holding one or more of the following positions in the 88th Congress: legislative or Appropriations Committee chairmen and ranking minority members; chairmen and ranking minority members of the subcommittees of the Appropriations Committee; the Speaker, the Majority Leader, a Majority Whip; and the Minority Leader, Minority Whip, and the Republican Conference Chairman.

In addition to the 110 respondents in these two samples, we interviewed the six Representatives in the "top leadership" of both parties who had not been selected for interviewing in either of the two random sampling procedures.[3] Although data from these six interviews appear nowhere in our quantitative analysis, they were invaluable as supplementary source material in our efforts to comprehend the role of the leadership in the politics of reform.

Table A-1 summarizes the composition of the three samples. It

TABLE A-1

Summary of the Three Completed Samples of Members of
the House of Representatives, 88th Congress

Sample		Democrats	Republicans	Sample totals
General	(nonleaders)	45	29	87
	(leaders)	8	5	
Leadership oversample		10	13	23
Top-leadership oversample		3	3	6
Party totals		66	50	116

should be noted that to produce these 116 completed interviews, stratified according to the appropriate party and leadership ratios, it was necessary to draw somewhat larger panels of potential respondents. A total of 132 Representatives were selected for interviewing. Of these, 118 (or 89.4 percent) were actually interviewed.[4]

As one might suspect, the completion rates were not uniform for the four groups of respondents. Table A-2 indicates that Republicans were somewhat more responsive to our requests for interviews than Democrats, although the latter could hardly be deemed uncooperative. And it was only among the Democrats that we

[3] Top formal leaders included the chairmen and ranking minority members of the committees on Appropriations, Ways and Means, and Rules, as well as the Speaker, Majority Leader, and Majority Whip and the Minority Leader, Minority Whip, and Republican Conference Chairman.

[4] Two of the interviews completed for the random sample were excluded from analysis because they would have served to overrepresent one of the party and leadership groups in the sample. The 89.4 percent completion rate compared favorably with the rates experienced in previous survey research in Congress (see Robinson, p. 225).

TABLE A-2

Interview–Panel Completion Rates by Party and Leadership Position

	Democrats	Republicans	Number in original panel
Nonleaders	90%	97%	81
Leaders	75%	96%	51
Number in original panel	78	54	132

actually experienced difficulty in gaining access to Representatives holding party- and committee-leadership positions.[5]

Interview-Schedule Construction and Administration

The intellectual origins of many of the questions in our interview schedule are not difficult to trace. We are heavily indebted to John C. Wahlke, Heinz Eulau, William Buchanan, and LeRoy C. Ferguson for the theoretical orientation—and in a number of cases the specific wording—of a number of the questions designed to elicit the role perceptions of Congressmen.[6] By gathering data on the normative and enacted roles of the members, we were able to focus upon that area we thought critical to an understanding of the internal politics of reform—the discrepancies perceived by Congressmen between the way they felt they (and the House) *ought* to act and the way they felt they (and the House) were *forced* to act, given the environment in which they operated.

The list of 32 reform proposals, to which we asked each of our respondents to react, was developed after a review of the extensive literature on Congress produced by political scientists, journalists, and members themselves. Bertram M. Gross' discussion of ''Significant Avenues of Procedural Reform'' was perhaps the single most fruitful inventory of suggestions for reform.[7]

The intensity scale that we employed to measure the strength of members' feelings for or against the reform proposals (see Appen-

[5] As far as we are able to discern, no systematic differences that would affect our analysis were found between the Democratic leaders we were able to interview and those we were not.

[6] See *The Legislative System*, Chaps. 1 and 11; Appendices 1 and 6.

[7] *The Legislative Struggle* (New York: McGraw-Hill, 1953), pp. 412–446.

dix B) was adapted from Donald R. Matthews' discussion of the concept of "activation" in his *U.S. Senators and Their World*.[8] The details of the administration of the survey instrument are too complex to be discussed fully here. However, a few comments may suggest the organization and costs of the research effort, as well as the quality of the data obtained.[9]

We pretested an early draft of the survey instrument during one week in April 1963. We discussed the questions in some detail with a number of congressional aides and with three Representatives who were known to have a greater-than-average interest in reform matters. In addition, we administered the pretest draft to a varied group of a half-dozen members who had little or no intellectual commitment to the subject of the research.

The final draft of the questionnaire was prepared in time for administration during the summer of 1963. More than two thirds of the interviews were conducted during July, August, and September; the balance were obtained during brief sorties to Washington that fall, and in the winter and spring of 1964. More than 50 percent of the interviews were conducted by one or another of the authors; another 10 percent were handled by our research assistant, James M. Hollabaugh, then a senior at Dartmouth College; the balance of the interviewing was done by eight Dartmouth students who were serving in Washington in the summer of 1963 as Dartmouth Public Service Interns.

Many tactics were employed to obtain the interviews. Initially, a letter of introduction and explanation was sent to each member whose name had been drawn for one of our samples. One of us would then make personal contact with the member's chief assistant in order to arrange an interview with the Representative. In a majority of cases, this procedure sufficed. In a few instances where no definite arrangements could be made after several telephone or personal contacts, we resorted to asking a friendly member to put in a word for us with the "fugitive" respondent. In short, we occasionally indulged in lobbying for access. But for the most part we relied upon the hospitality of Congressmen—and upon our own patience and persistence as well.

[8] (Chapel Hill: University of North Carolina Press, 1960), pp. 192–193.

[9] Fuller treatments of the tactics of survey interviewing among members of Congress may be found in Robinson, pp. 222–234, and in Charles O. Jones, "Notes on Interviewing Members of the House of Representatives," *Public Opinion Quarterly*, 23 (Fall 1959), 404–406.

Virtually all interviewing was carried out in the privacy of the members' inner offices. Occasionally interviews were conducted in the Rayburn reception room adjacent to the floor of the House or over a meal in the House restaurant. Interviews varied in length from 20 minutes to over four hours. The mean elapsed time was 55 minutes. It is estimated that in excess of 500 man-hours were devoted to the process of arranging and conducting the 118 interviews.

Interview Schedule

On the face sheet of the schedule were recorded the interview number, the interviewer's name, and the date and length of the interview. Also appearing on this sheet was an explanation of the study, which the interviewer was instructed to relate but not read to the respondent. The interview followed this explanation.

> As you know, many people *outside* of Capitol Hill have been interested in the subject of congressional organization and procedure. You hear in the press almost constant criticism about the way Congress operates. And academic people have been talking about congressional reform for many years. We thought it was about time that somebody tried in a systematic way to ask *Congressmen* about their attitudes toward these issues.
> With this in mind, some of us at Dartmouth College are conducting a survey of the attitudes of Congressmen toward House organization. We want to find out what aspects of your job you feel are most important. We also want to know which things in the House seem to make your job easier, and which things make it harder. We have selected about 100 Congressmen whom we are to interview. Your name has been selected, and we very much appreciate your willingness to participate in our study. I want to emphasize that this interview will be considered strictly confidential, and that your responses will be averaged with those of your colleagues. And I also want to assure you that we have no axes to grind; we are not in any way advocating or campaigning for reform. We simply feel that the views of Congressmen themselves have not been adequately explored in the press and elsewhere. And we would like to remedy this situation.

(Note: interviewer instructions are enclosed in brackets.)

   1. I'd like to start by asking a couple of questions about the job of being a Congressman:
      a. First of all, how would you describe the job of being a Congressman—what are the most important things you should do here? [*Probe as fully as possible. If there is a difference*

*between what he does and what he thinks he should be doing,
explore adequately and get both. If no indication of such,
probe to see if ideal and actual roles are in harmony.*]

  b. Now, what are the most pressing problems you face in trying
     to do your job as Congressman—what are the things that
     hinder you in your tasks? [*Try to get beyond such general
     statements as "lack of time"; get the specific things which
     prevent R from doing his job the way he would like to.*]

2. Now let's turn briefly to the role of Congress *as a whole* and its
   place in our government:

  a. First, what role should Congress play in our governmental
     system—what should its functions be? [*Probe as fully as
     possible. We are anxious to get at perceptions of the role of
     Congress vis-a-vis the President in legislation and adminis-
     tration, and in regard to the representative functions of
     Congress. Probe also for perceptions of the role of the House
     as opposed to the Senate.*]

  b. How effective is Congress (and especially the House) in
     fulfilling the role(s) you feel it should play? [*Probe to get
     specific failures of Congress, if R has any on his mind.*]

  c. [*If R sees any discrepancy between what Congress ought to
     do and what it does:*] What are the most pressing problems
     which prevent Congress from doing what you think it ought
     to do?

3. To go a little further with this question, we have collected some
   statements that Congressmen and others have made about the
   nature of Congressional life. You may very well find some of
   these to be quite oversimplified, particularly since they deal
   with complex subjects. But we would like your general reaction
   to each one. These are all matters of opinion so there are no
   correct or incorrect answers. [*Hand R question 3.*] Would you
   please read each statement and then check the response which
   best indicates your agreement or disagreement with the statement. (Note: respondents could choose among "agree," "tend
   to agree," "undecided," "tend to disagree," and "disagree.")

  (1) Congress should devote its time to broad policy questions
      rather than the details of administration.

  (2) Under our form of government every individual should
      take an interest in government directly, not through a
      political party.

  (3) Congressmen should educate the public to help citizens
      understand issues so they can form opinions and make
      their opinions known.

  (4) The structure of Congress should be designed to protect
      minority interests from being overrun by hasty majorities.

  (5) If a bill is important for his party's record, a member
      should vote with his party even if it costs him some sup-
      port in his district.

  (6) A Congressman ought to decide how to vote on most is-

sues by asking himself if the proposed law is morally right.

(7) The primary function of House rules and structure must be to allow the majority to work its will.

(8) The two parties should take clear-cut, opposing stands on more of the important and controversial issues.

(9) A Representative ought to work for what his constituents want even though this may not always agree with his personal views.

(10) Congress should play the major role in the making of public policy.

(11) When you come to Washington you have great ideas. But when you are in a committee or on the floor, you are unable to implement your ideas.

(12) On the whole, Congress would work better if there were no interest groups and lobbies trying to influence legislation.

(13) An important part of a Congressman's job should be to go to bat for constituents in their dealings with executive agencies.

(14) Congress and the executive should be equal partners in making of public policy.

(15) Issues are so technical and time is so short that I often vote without adequate knowledge of the issue.

(16) The job of the Congressman should be to work out compromises among conflicting interests.

(17) I seldom have to sound out my constituents because I think so much like them that I know how to react to almost any proposal.

(18) The executive should play the major role in the making of public policy.

(19) So many groups and individuals want so many different things that it is often difficult to know what stand to take.

(20) Lobbyists and special interests have entirely too much influence in the House.

(21) As a Congressman I can do pretty much what I like here without worrying too much about criticism from my district.

(22) Congress should take an active part in overseeing the administration of public policy.

(23) The best interests of the people would be better served if Congressmen were elected without party labels.

(24) Congress should equip itself with a more extensive professional staff, in order to have its own sources of technical knowledge on the complex problems confronting the nation.

(25) Under our form of government, every individual should seek to influence his Congressman directly, rather than through interest groups and organizations.

(26) The function of Congress should be to ratify or modify legislative proposals initiated by the executive.

4. Here is a short list of proposals that Congressmen and others have made for possible changes in congressional organization and procedure. Some of these proposals may seem to you to be radical; others may sound helpful; some may seem trivial. We are anxious to get your reactions to all these proposals. [*Hand R booklet containing question 4.*] Please read each of the proposals in the list and circle your impressions on the two scales which accompany each proposal. If you have any further comments on these proposals I'd be glad to hear them as you go along. (Note: the 32 proposals and the accompanying scales are in Appendix B.)

5. [*After R has completed question 4:*] Are there any other specific changes *not* on this list which you would like to mention— either changes you favor or those which you have heard about but do not favor? [*If R mentions any other reforms:*] Using the same scales as appear on the list, what position would you probably take on the proposal? How likely is the House to adopt this proposal within the next ten years?

6. Have you personally discussed with any of your colleagues here in the House any of the proposals on the list (or any of those you have added)?
   [*If "yes":*]
   a. Which proposals were involved?
   b. Who was involved in the discussion?
   c. What was said?
   d. What has come of it?

7. Do you happen to know whether any (other) members of the House are now working actively for or against these measures?
   [*If "yes":*]
   a. Which proposals are involved?
   b. Who is involved?
   c. What are they doing?

8. Have you had any contact with persons or groups outside the House in regard to any of these proposals?
   [*If "yes":*]
   a. Which proposals were involved?
   b. Who was involved? Are they from your district?
   c. What was said?
   d. Has anything come of it?

9. Is there anything else about this subject that you think we ought to explore in our study?

B.

CONGRESSIONAL ATTITUDES TOWARD CONGRESSIONAL REORGANIZATION

In question 4 of the survey instrument, House members were presented with a list of 32 proposals for changing the organization and operation of the House of Representatives. These proposals, listed in Table B-1, were selected to represent most of the major areas of congressional activity that have been the subject of criticism by political scientists, journalists, and members themselves over the past two decades. For each proposal, Congressmen were requested to respond in two ways. They were first instructed as follows:

> Given the intensity of your feelings for or against this proposal and the probable "costs" that your action might impose on you— that is, the possible difficulties of taking a position—circle the position on Scale A below which best describes the most active position you would probably be willing to take on this proposal.

Scale A then followed:

Would lead fight AGAINST	Would work AGAINST	Would tell other Con- gressmen I'm AGAINST	Would likely vote AGAINST	Would likely vote FOR	Would tell other Con- gressmen I'm FOR	Would work FOR	Would lead fight FOR

The position on the scale selected by the Representative not only indicated whether his attitude was favorable or unfavorable but also provided a measure of the intensity of his attitude—as indicated by his likely behavior.

The Congressmen were next asked:

> How likely is the House to adopt this proposal within the next ten years? Circle the position on Scale B below which best expresses your impression of this probability.

Scale B appeared as follows:

Extremely Unlikely			Fifty-fifty			Extremely Likely
↓			↓			↓
1	2	3	4	5	6	7

These two scales permit a comparison between how the Congressmen felt about each proposal and their predictions of the likelihood of each proposal's adoption.

The responses for each proposal are presented in simplified form in Table B-1. In Scale A—the activity scale—the respondents who selected either "talking," "working," or "leading the fight for or against" are reported as "Strongly For" and "Strongly Against," respectively. Those respondents who chose either of the "voting" positions are reported as "For" or "Against."

In Scale B, the two extreme positions ("Extremely Unlikely" and "Extremely Likely") and the midpoint ("Fifty-fifty") are reported as they were in the questionnaire; the respondents choosing positions 2 or 3 are reported as "Unlikely"; those choosing 5 or 6 are reported as "Likely."

The data in Table B-1 are from the general sample of the House. The proposals are arrayed in the descending order of support that they received.

TABLE B-1

Congressional Attitudes toward Congressional Reorganization: Probable Activity and Estimates of Likelihood of Adoption*

Proposal	SCALE A: ACTIVITY						SCALE B: LIKELIHOOD					
	Strongly for	For	Against	Strongly against	Totals %	(N)	Extremely likely	Likely	50-50	Unlikely	Extremely unlikely	Totals % (N)
1. Authorize the General Accounting Office to review all budget requests after they are submitted by the President, and increase the GAO's responsibility for reporting regularly to Congress on its audits of expenditures.	38%	48%	11%	4%	101%	(75)**	1%	15%	31%	43%	11%	101 (75)
2. Increase each member's clerk-hire allowance to permit the hiring of an Administrative Assistant, in accordance with Senate practice under the Legislative Reorganization Act of 1946.	52	31	13	4	100	(82)	17	31	36	12	4	100 (81)
3. Establish a joint committee to study the reorganization of Congress.	42	36	15	7	100	(83)	9	24	38	22	7	100 (81)

* Based upon a random sample of 87 members of the House of Representatives, 88th Congress. Techniques for determining a member's probable activity for or against each of the reform proposals and his estimates of the likelihood of House adoption of the proposals are explained in the preceding pages.

** Differences between the number of members reacting to any one proposal and the number of members in the general sample (87) are caused by "don't know" responses and by the failure of a few members to respond to some of the proposals.

SCALE A: ACTIVITY SCALE B: LIKELIHOOD

Proposal	Strongly for	For	Against	Strongly against	Totals % (N)	Extremely likely	Likely	50–50	Unlikely	Extremely unlikely	Totals % (N)
4. Formally designate specific days for floor business and committee business, increasing the days for floor business as the session proceeds.	36%	39%	17%	8%	100% (76)	1%	9%	29%	43%	17%	99 (75)
5. Create a "Joint Committee on Fiscal Policy," composed of members of House and Senate appropriations and revenue committees to give broad consideration and direction to federal spending.	42	31	19	8	100 (78)	1	16	36	34	13	100 (77)
6. Schedule year-long congressional sessions with specified periodic recesses.	40	29	21	10	100 (80)	3	22	28	34	13	100 (77)
7. Increase terms of the members of the House to four years, the members to be elected at the time of the presidential elections.	44	24	6	27	101 (85)	1	5	17	39	38	100 (82)
8. Reformulate committee jurisdictions to reduce overlap and to correspond more precisely with executive departments and agencies.	30	37	27	6	100 (78)	1	13	29	33	23	99 (75)
9. Permit the House, by majority vote, to require the executive branch to pro-	38	22	19	22	101 (79)	1	9	20	34	36	100 (76)

vide information requested by any committee.

10. Allow the ranking minority member of each committee to hire staff members roughly in proportion to his party's representation on the committee.	34	26	22	18	100 (80)	1	14	31	42	12	100 (78)
11. Empower House committees to authorize broadcasting or telecasting of hearings by majority vote of the committee.	26	32	12	30	100 (84)	4	12	40	31	13	100 (83)
12. Establish party policy committees, composed of the primary elective leaders and the chairman (or ranking minority member) from each committee, to set legislative priorities and determine party strategy.	16	42	28	14	100 (76)	1	9	26	42	22	100 (74)
13. Publish committee votes on bills and amendments upon request of one fifth of the members of that committee.	25	32	26	17	100 (81)	2	10	18	46	24	100 (79)
14. Reinstate the so-called "21-day rule," under which the chairman of a committee that favorably reported a bill could call it up for House consideration if the Rules Committee reported adversely or failed to act upon it within 21 days.	26	27	20	27	100 (78)	1	4	30	36	29	100 (76)
15. Remove District of Columbia affairs from congressional jurisdiction.	28	20	28	24	100 (82)	1	15	32	30	22	100 (78)

SCALE A: ACTIVITY   SCALE B: LIKELIHOOD

Proposal	Strongly for	For	Against	Strongly against	Totals % (N)	Extremely likely	Likely	50–50	Unlikely	Extremely unlikely	Totals % (N)
16. Establish a nonpartisan, career, "congressional civil service" staff of high professional competence—administered impartially and assigned to standing committees.	15%	33%	27%	25%	100 (82)	3%	5%	21%	38%	33%	100 (78)
17. Appropriate funds for federal agencies and programs on a two-year basis and devote the alternate years largely to review and oversight.	17	28	31	24	100 (82)	3	3	16	40	39	101 (80)
18. Limit the jurisdiction of the Rules Committee to that of determining the type of rule and the length of debate to be granted to bills reported by standing committees.	28	15	22	35	100 (82)	1	12	18	41	8	100 (78)
19. On the floor of the House, use electronic voting devices, which would record a member's vote on any measure on which one fifth of the members present request such a vote (that is, the present requirement for a roll-call vote).	23	18	18	42	101 (84)	1	6	9	29	55	100 (84)
20. Assign responsibility for editing verbatim floor remarks to the Government Printing Office, and relegate to	17	22	29	32	100 (77)	1	8	13	45	33	100 (77)

The appendix text (continuation of item 20) and numbered proposals 21–26, with two sets of response distributions (each summing to ~100%, year in parentheses).

Item / Proposal					Total						Total
… the appendix of the *Congressional Record* all remarks not actually delivered on the House floor.											
21. Require present House and Senate standing committees to conduct joint hearings on all executive-initiated legislation, unless such hearings are opposed by majority vote in either committee.	8	30	43	19	100 (79)	0	5	11	40	44	100 (78)
22. Enforce a rule reducing a member's salary in proportion to his absence from formal House responsibilities—House sessions and committee meetings—with exceptions made for illness and similar unavoidable conditions.	12	23	33	32	100 (82)	1	5	4	21	69	100 (78)
23. Reorganize the standing committees so that the same committee will have responsibility for the authorization, appropriation, and investigation of policy in a given subject-matter area.	17	16	36	31	100 (81)	1	6	10	42	41	100 (79)
24. Replace present standing committees with joint committees wherever feasible.	7	24	33	35	99 (82)	0	4	6	35	55	100 (80)
25. Provide for periodic appearances of executive officials of cabinet rank on the House floor to answer questions submitted in writing by members.	13	17	43	27	100 (82)	1	3	11	33	53	101 (80)
26. Select committee chairmen for each Congress by the party caucus, from the three senior (majority) members of each committee.	13	16	25	46	100 (83)	1	2	4	30	63	100 (81)

SCALE A: ACTIVITY   SCALE B: LIKELIHOOD

Proposal	Strongly for	For	Against	Strongly against	Totals %	(N)	Extremely likely	Likely	50–50	Unlikely	Extremely unlikely	Totals %	(N)
27. Reduce the number of signatures needed for a discharge petition to 150 (from present 218).	16%	11%	25%	48%	100	(83)	3%	3%	10%	36%	49%	101	(80)
28. Empower party policy committees to control committee assignments of new and returning members at beginning of each Congress in order to encourage party unity.	8	19	29	44	100	(73)	1	7	11	36	44	99	(70)
29. Select the chairman of each standing committee by vote of the majority-party members of the committee.	9	12	36	43	100	(81)	0	5	6	30	59	100	(78)
30. Continue the present system of selecting committee chairmen by seniority, but permit no member to serve as chairman in more than one out of three Congresses.	9	8	29	54	100	(79)	1	1	4	29	65	100	(77)
31. Appropriate by means of a single, omnibus appropriations bill.	10	5	30	55	100	(82)	0	2	4	31	63	100	(81)
32. Require members to forfeit seniority privileges after each six consecutive terms.	5	9	33	53	100	(81)	0	1	3	23	73	100	(78)

C.

REPORT OF THE 1965 JOINT COMMITTEE ON THE ORGANIZATION OF THE CONGRESS

On July 21, 1966, at a press conference in the sedate old Supreme Court Chamber in the Capitol, the Joint Committee on the Organization of the Congress announced its approval of a final report. Before klieg lights, television-news cameras, several dozen reporters, and scores of onlookers, the Co-Chairmen—Senator A. S. Mike Monroney and Representative Ray J. Madden—and the ranking committee Republicans—Senator Karl Mundt and Representative Thomas B. Curtis—exchanged the pleasantries indigenous to all congressional press performances and proceeded to read from prepared summaries of the committee recommendations and supplemental minority views.

Among its nearly 50 recommendations, the report proposed several revisions in the standing-committee system—the basic working unit of Congress. It recommended a "bill of rights" for committees that would give a majority of each committee's membership the right to call meetings and report legislation in the event that a chairman refuses to do so. It suggested more frequent use of open hearings and the telecasting or broadcasting of committee deliberations—at the option of the committee. Safeguards were prescribed to insure that all committee members might participate in the preparation of committee reports and that such reports be made available to all members prior to floor action. The report suggested the elimination of the use of proxy voting in committees.

Several changes in committee structure and jurisdiction were recommended, including the creation of new Committees on Education in each House. These new committees would assume the educational jurisdiction of the Senate Committee on Labor and Public Welfare and the House Committee on Education and Labor, as well as other educational programs under the jurisdiction of other committees.

The joint committee report recommended an attempt to achieve a better distribution of workload in the Senate by placing a limitation on the number of committee assignments and chairmanships a member may hold. It also recommended that a Senator not serve on more than one of the following major committees: Appropriations, Finance, Foreign Relations and Armed Services.

The joint committee proposed that committee staff resources be considerably expanded and improved. Three positions—two professional and one clerical—would be assigned to each committee's minority representation upon its request. An additional staff member designated as a "review specialist" would be assigned to each standing committee to review the administration of existing laws.

The report made a number of recommendations in the field of fiscal controls and congressional review of the budget. It urged the use of automatic data processing to expand budget information available to members. Specific changes in the presentation of the budget were suggested. The joint committee recommended that within 30 days after submission of the budget executive-budget officials appear before the full Appropriations Committees of each House to discuss overall budget guidelines. The Appropriations Committees were encouraged to expand their study of multi-agency programs and to hold more hearings. The joint-committee report proposed new operating units within the General Accounting Office to assist committees in program evaluation.

The joint committee asked that each member of congress have a personal legislative assistant. The Legislative Reference Service, to be renamed the "Legislative Research Service," was marked for expansion.

The report urged that congressional business be scheduled throughout a five-day work week. A roll-call vote would be necessary to extend a session beyond July 31st, and no session would be held in August except in time of war.

The *Congressional Record* would be altered in content and format. For example, it was recommended that the body of the *Record* be limited to germane insertions and verbatim remarks actually delivered. Nongermane debate would be printed in a separate section.

The joint committee encouraged the House to follow the Senate in establishing a Committee on Standards and Conduct. Members were urged to divest themselves of patronage responsibilities in the appointment of postmasters and rural mail carriers. A number of recommendations were made for the centralization and professionalization of certain Capitol "housekeeping" functions.

Finally, the report recommended the creation of a Joint Committee on Congressional Operations to conduct continuing studies of the organization and operations of Congress—in some respects serving as a permanent successor to the Joint Committee on the Organization of the Congress.

The report was unanimously approved by the joint committee, although a number of supplemental views, principally from Republican members, were filed. These included proposals for minority-party control of an investigatory committee when the same party controls both houses of Congress and the Presidency; curbs on administrative lobbying by the executive branch; disclosure of assets and income by members; and proposals relating to the financing of political campaigns. Congressman Ken Hechler (D-W. Va.) called for reforms going considerably beyond the committee report, including provision for electronic voting on an optional basis.

Co-Chairman Monroney expressed cautious confidence that the recommendations embodied in the report, presented to the House and Senate as an omnibus "Legislative Reorganization Act of 1966," would be acted upon before the adjournment of the 89th Congress.

The tone of the questions from newsmen was distinctly critical. The Co-Chairmen were asked why the joint committee had not recommended revisions in the seniority system, the filibuster, the retirement of aged members, campaign finance, ethics, and the proliferation of subcommittees. Senator Monroney defended the scope of the report by pointing to the constraints in the mandate originally given the joint committee (it was barred from making changes in House or Senate rules), the political realities of reform, and the argument that "change is a mosiac of little reforms." When asked whether he thought the joint-committee recommendations met the challenge laid down by critics of congressional operations, and if the report amounted to "anything substantial," the Oklahoma Democrat admitted that the report lacked "the spectacular appeal of the 1946 Reorganization Act." One Congressman close to the work of the joint committee privately commented that the report reflected "the very weakness of the Congress. By and large, all [the committee] did was to exhort the Congress to do what it has always had the power and the obligation to do anyway.''

In Chapter 5, we identified two major types of structural and procedural innovation: (1) the relatively noncontroversial changes designed to increase the ''efficiency'' of Congress, and (2) those innovations aimed at enhancing the position of party, policy, or institutional power blocs. The 1966 report of the joint committee reflected primarily the ''efficiency'' motif. Without any consensus on a thoroughgoing conception of congressional functioning, reforms of political necessity were largely limited to small steps presumably designed to increase access to information, to expedite the work of congressional office and committee staffs, and generally to render the life of the Congressman a bit more tolerable.

But there were power stakes dimly perceivable in the joint committee's recommendations. The minority party's position was strengthened by increasing and regularizing its information-gathering facilities. And, if adopted, many of the reforms might well enhance the power of Congress *vis-a-vis* the executive by facilitating Congress' activities in lawmaking, consensus building, and oversight—all primary functions in the literary theory of Congress.

Over the long haul, the proposed permanent Joint Committee on Congressional Operations, if adequately staffed and funded and not tightly restricted in the scope of its activities, might be the most significant of the reforms emanating from the Monroney-Madden committee. As an institutionalized means of ''preventive maintenance,'' such a body could serve a strengthened Congress by continuous and thorough thinking and research about change—before change occurs unnoticed, or before it is forced upon Congress in an era distinctly hostile to the national legislature.

INDEX

310